Growing Irises

Growing Irises

G.E. Cassidy and S. Linnegar

'Thou art the Iris,
fair among the fairest'

Longfellow.

CROOM HELM   London & Sydney
TIMBER PRESS   Portland, Oregon

© 1982 G.E. Cassidy and S. Linnegar
Croom Helm Ltd, Provident House, Burrell Row,
Beckenham, Kent BR3 1AT

British Library Cataloguing in Publication Data

Cassidy, G.E.
   Growing irisis.
   1. Iris (Plant)
   I. Title II. Linnegar
   635.9'3424   SB413.18
   ISBN 0-7099-0706-0

Reprinted 1985

Published in North America by Timber Press,
PO Box 1631
Beaverton, Oregon 97075
USA
ISBN 0-917304-42-X

Printed and bound in Great Britain by
Biddles Ltd, Guildford and King's Lynn

Contents

List of Figures

Figures

Acknowledgements

We acknowledge with gratitude the encouragement and advice of many members of the British Iris Society. Our special thanks are due to Mrs G.R. Tallack and Mrs T.A. Blanco White, to Stephen Drury and Gordon Rowley of the University of Reading and to Jack Venner, for his advice on American irises.

For photographs our thanks go to Jan Dickson, D.H. Goodwin, M. Halliwell, A. Mumford, Mrs Laura M. Reid and W.F. Worth. Finally, we are very grateful to Christopher Helm for giving us the opportunity of proving that our friendship could survive a collaboration.

G.E.C.
S.L.

Line drawings by G.E. Cassidy

CHAPTER 1

The Story of the Iris

Our main purpose in writing this book is not to provide a highly scientific account of the genus *Iris* but to try to pass on something of our love and enthusiasm for this beautiful flower and to demonstrate how it can be used, in many seasons and in varying conditions, to enhance the delight of our gardens.

Perhaps we should at once clear up the age-old misconception that the iris is just a flower for the early summer — for nothing could be further from the truth. Indeed there is probably no genus of hardy plants that can provide flowers in the garden for as many months of the year as do irises. As witness of this, W.R. Dykes himself, the legendary hero of the iris world, became fascinated by the genus largely because it was the only one which gave him flowers in the winter months in his garden in Surrey. The plain fact is that, with reasonable care, it is possible to have one kind of iris or another in flower for some eight or nine months of the year.

Most irises are exceedingly beautiful and some, indeed, have no rivals in point of sheer beauty of form and colour and there are few plants which can vie with the iris for the number of its good qualities. Many irises are so easy to grow that success is assured for any gardener in any kind of garden. Others present difficulties which worthily excite the continual perseverance of the most skilful and offer a rich reward to those who attain success. It is a genus *par excellence* alike for the average gardener and for the intellectual specialist. Before dealing with the many uses of the iris in our gardens we should give some account of the flower itself, its special character, traditional uses and long and interesting history.

The genus *Iris* is part of the large family of flowering plants named Iridaceae which includes also the crocus, gladiolus, ixia and freesia. It comprises some 200 species, all with flowers made up of parts in sets of three, but with botanical differences in the plants which enable them to be distinguished in separate groups. The flowers themselves are miraculously contrived by nature to ensure survival. They consist of six segments, popularly known as 'standards' and 'falls', which rise from a perianth tube at the base of which is the ovary. (Figure 1.1) In addition to these six segments there are three

The Iris
Described

11

Figure 1.1
Outline Drawing to
Explain the
Terminology Used to
Denote the Various
Parts of the Iris
Flower

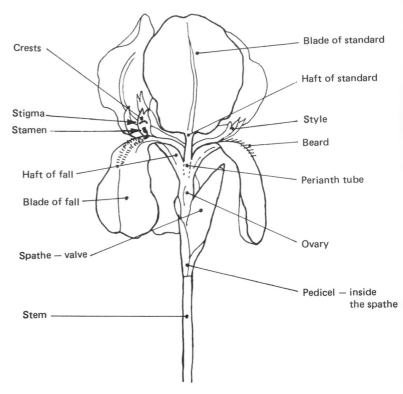

Crests

Blade of standard

Haft of standard

Stigma

Stamen

Style

Beard

Haft of fall

Blade of fall

Perianth tube

Spathe — valve

Ovary

Stem

Pedicel — inside
the spathe

style branches which arch over the anthers and bear on their underside, near the extremity, the stigmatic surface through which the
flower is fertilised. The style branches form the roof, and the haft of
the falls the floor, of a kind of tunnel. The stigma projects downwards at the mouth of this tunnel along the roof of which lie the
anthers. These bear the pollen and at their base exudes the nectar.
This symmetrical arrangement, thus rather prosaically described, in
fact produces a flower of the greatest beauty and elegance of form.
The flowers appear in a wide range of colours, with a variety of
intermingling of the colours within that range and many forms of
veining and stippling. On a number of the species a distinctive
feature is the line of coloured hairs on the central line of the falls at
the heart of the flower which is known as the beard and may be of
matching or contrasting shade. All this results in a showy flower of
great attraction, and we may well ask what the meaning is of such a
showy creation. As in the case of every other flower, its object is to
set seed and reproduce itself, and the showiness is designed to attract
the insects, mainly bees, which will further this purpose. Pollen has
to be carried from one flower to another and the bees must be

attracted to the flowers, first by the colours, and then by the hope of reward from the nectar they obtain. So we see that a bee of the right size, pressing down the tunnel below the arch of the style arm, must necessarily sweep off on its back some of the pollen from the anther, exactly placed for the purpose. On entering another flower it must necessarily leave some of the pollen on the stigmatic lip, again exactly contrived for the purpose, and pollination is achieved. But, of course, bees do not always obligingly stick to the rules. They are apt to take a short cut to the nectar if they can and they do not confine themselves to one species of flower. They cannot, therefore, be relied upon to fertilise all irises and certain species survive only because they have a slightly different formation which makes self-pollination possible. Moreover, bees do not keep records of where they have been and, although they were relied on by hybridisers until quite late in the last century, later hybridisers have adopted the more prosaic but safer method of manual pollination. In studying the arrangement of the flower we must realise that it is remarkably perfect and feel a sense of wonder at the process of evolution which has resulted in a form at once so beautiful and so perfectly adapted for the job of perpetuating the genus.

The species of the genus *Iris* can be conveniently divided into Classification
bulbous and *non-bulbous*.
  The bulbous irises are subdivided into three groups:

(1) the Xiphiums, which comprise the Dutch, Spanish and English irises, well known as florists' flowers,
(2) the early flowering and small Reticulatas,
(3) the Junos, which are distinguished by the fact that the bulbs, in their resting state, have attached to their base a number of fleshy tuberous roots.

Almost all bulbous irises are beardless.
  The non-bulbous irises have for their rootstock what is known as a rhizome, which is really a horizontal creeping stem. This stem has a system of roots pushing down from its underside and produces a fan of leaves and a flower stem pushing upwards from one end. This rhizome is capable of extension by means of lateral shoots so that rhizomatous irises can spread far more easily than the bulbous ones. When the creeping stem has thrown up its flower and completed its task, its growth ceases and the energy of the plant is diverted to the production of lateral buds. These can usually be found on either side of the rhizome near the base of the tuft of leaves. From these buds fresh rhizomes form and it is from these that the flower stems arise

Figure 1.2
Forms of the
Flowers of the Iris

Bearded iris
I.trojana

Oncocyclus iris
I.lortetii

Spuria iris
I.aurea

in the following season.

The non-bulbous, or rhizomatous irises are also naturally divided into three groups:

(1) *Bearded irises*, which normally have broad leaves and large, hard and fleshy rhizomes proportionate to their height. They are called pogon irises and comprise the true bearded types and three additional groups, Oncocyclus, Regelia and Pseudo-regelia.

(2) *Beardless irises*, which normally have narrower leaves and smaller, fibrous rhizomes. They comprise a wide range of species which include Sibirica, Spuria, Japanese and Californian and a number of individually classified plants.

(3) *Crested irises*, which have thin rhizomes and a conspicuous ridge or crest along the centre line of the falls.

Just to be perverse *I. collettii* and *I. decora* are neither bulbous nor rhizomatous but grow from a bunch of fleshy roots, and have their own special sub-genus, *nepalensis*. For horticultural purposes, in nurserymen's lists and for showing, bearded irises have for many years been divided into three groups, dwarf, intermediate and tall. With the development of many new variations in the intermediate range a more precise grouping has become essential and new standards have been introduced in the USA and are now almost universally recognised. They are based on the size and characteristics of the plants and their flowering times:

Miniature Dwarf Bearded (MDB) up to 20 cm (8 ins). They usually have unbranched stems and flowers 5-8 cm (2-3 ins) across and are the first of the bearded irises to come into bloom.

Standard Dwarf Bearded (SDB) between 21 and 40 cm (8 and 15 ins). They usually have branched stems and flowers 8-10 cm (3-4 ins) across. In this range the hybrids from first and later generations of crosses between tall bearded irises and *I.pumila* are known as lilliputs. SDBs flower after the MDBs.

Intermediate Bearded (IB) between 41 and 70 cm (16 and 27 ins). They have flowers 10-13 cm (4-5 ins) across and their flowering period is between the SDBs and the TBs.

Miniature Tall Bearded (MTB) between 41 and 70 cm (16 and 27 ins). They are indeed miniature versions of tall bearded irises with flowers not more than 15 cm (6 ins) combined height and width, borne on well-branched, slender stems. They come into bloom at

Bulb of *I.reticulata*
with netted covering

Bulb of Juno iris
with fleshy roots

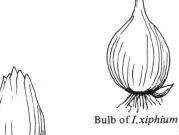

Figure 1.3
Bulbs and
Rootstocks (not
to scale)

Bulb of *I.xiphium*

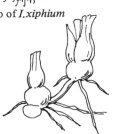

Regelia iris with
new rhizome from
underground stolon

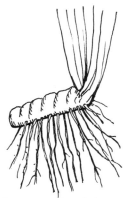

Rhizome of bearded
iris

Rhizome of *I.spuria*

Rhizome of
I.sibirica

Roots of
I. decora

Surface stolon of
I.cristata

the same time as the TBs.

Border Bearded (BB) between 41 and 70 cm (16 and 27 ins). They have flowers 10-13 cm (4-5 ins) across and bloom with the TBs of which they are smaller versions.

Tall Bearded (TB) more than 70 cm (27 ins). They have flowers 10-18 cm (4-7 ins) across and are the last of the bearded irises to come into bloom.

(For the benefit of the specialist and the more enquiring gardener we include as Appendix VI a fully developed classification of the genus.)

Distribution

It is important for gardeners to know where the plants originally came from so that they can provide them with the growing conditions in which they are likely to flourish. Although irises are now grown under cultivation throughout the world, they are native only to the northern temperate zone and the natural habitats of the various species can be closely defined.

The larger bulbous irises (*I.xiphium*) came from Southern Spain, Portugal, Southern France and the North coast of Africa, though

Figure 1.4
Classification of
Bearded Irises

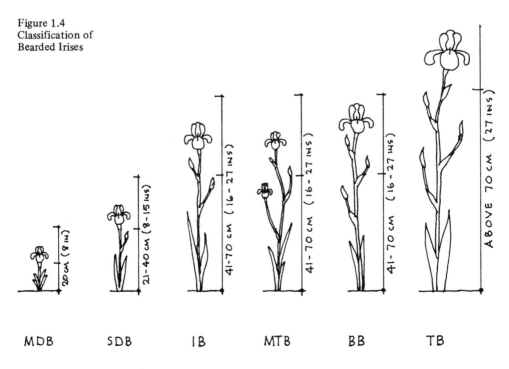

Figure 1.5 World Distribution of Irises

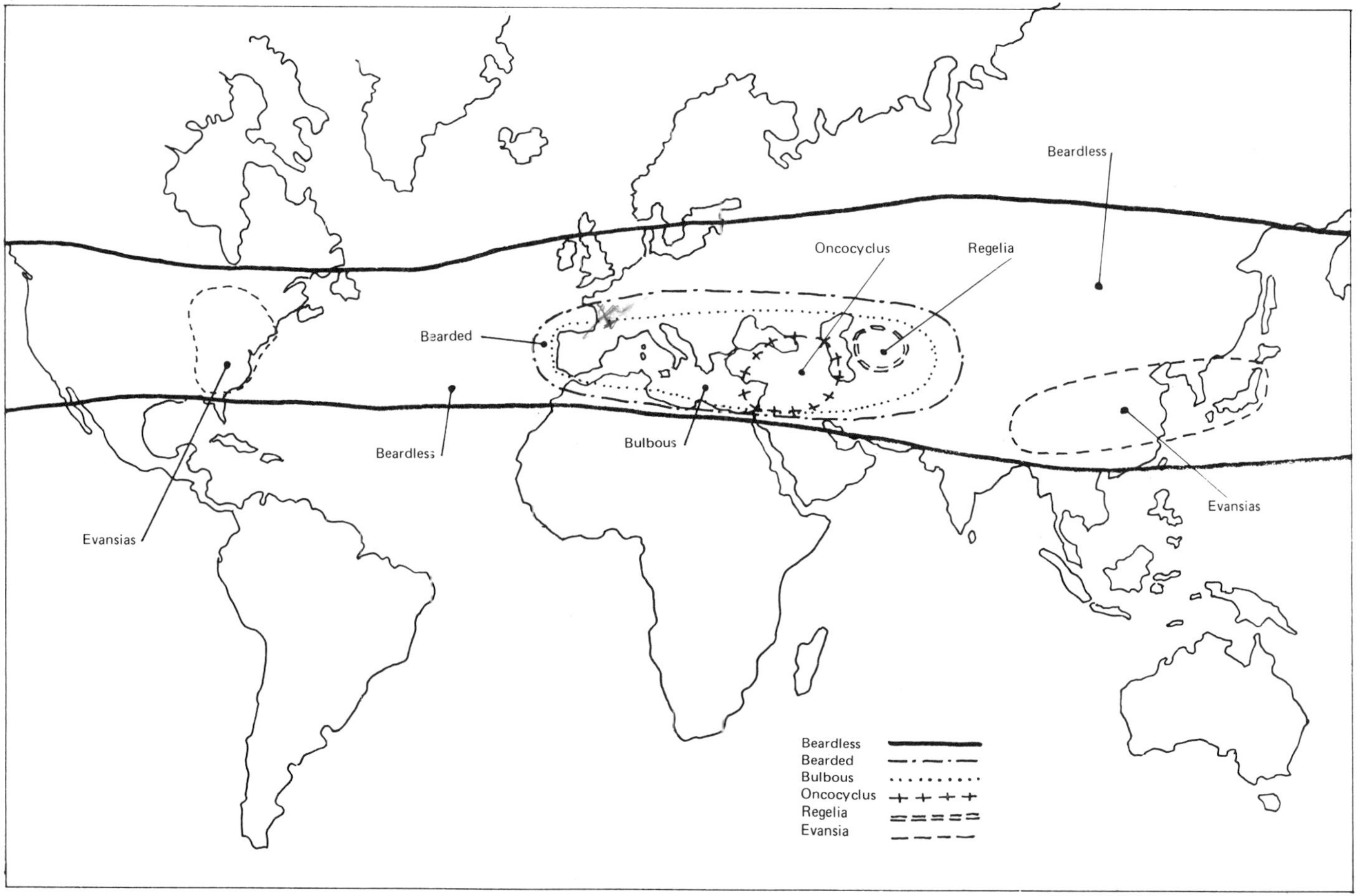

the names they bear, Dutch, English and Spanish may seem misleading. 'Dutch irises' were hybrids produced early in the century by the Hoog Brothers of the Dutch firm of Van Tubergen by crossing the Spanish irises with other species. This resulted in a larger and finer flower of which a number of varieties exist which are widely used in commerce as florists' flowers. 'English irises' are descendants of *I.xiphioides* (now known as *I.latifolia*) native of the Pyrenees. They were apparently brought to Bristol, centuries ago, by merchant seamen and being there discovered by gardeners were thought to be native to the area and were called 'English irises'. The Reticulatas came from an area spreading from the eastern Mediterranean through Iran to southern Russia. The *Junos* are native of a wider area spanning from Spain and North Africa, eastwards through the middle eastern countries to southern Russia and the west of India.

The tall bearded irises derived originally from a comparatively small area of central and southern Europe and the Eastern Mediterranean. For many years it was mistakenly thought that the common 'flag', *I.germanica* or German iris, was the ancestor of all the modern hybrids. Why it came to be known as germanica we cannot tell for it has never been found growing wild in Germany. Nor is it a true species, but an almost sterile hybrid probably of *I.aphylla* and *I.variegata*. Because of the vigour of its growth it has always been the commonest and easiest to grow of all irises and was naturally assumed to be the progenitor of all the rest. In fact the modern TB was derived ultimately from two species, *I.pallida*, native of the country between the South Tyrol and the Dalmatian coast and *I.variegata*, which extends from south Austria right through the Balkans.

The smaller bearded species are native of southern France, northern Italy, the Balkans and southern Russia.

The exotic Oncocyclus and Regelias come from the arid regions of Palestine, Israel, Iran, Afghanistan and southern Russia.

The beardless irises come from more widely spread environments.

In broad terms the Sibiricas are native of central Europe and Asia; the Spurias of central and eastern Europe, southern Asia and north west India; the Californias, Louisianas, Longipetalas and a number of allied species, of the southern USA; the Laevigatas span the northern hemisphere and the Evansias, the crested irises, come from eastern Asia and the eastern USA.

Individual species which have specially interesting areas of distribution should be mentioned. *I.unguicularis*, the winter-flowering iris known more commonly as *I.stylosa*, comes from Algeria and the north eastern Mediterranean; *I.versicolor*, a self-fertilising species and the source of 'blue flag' root, is widely distributed on the eastern side of North America from Hudson Bay to Texas; *I.cristata*, the tiny sweetly-scented crested iris, is from the eastern USA. Finally, *I.pseudacorus*, the wild yellow flag and *I.foetidissima*, the evergreen 'stinking iris', are spread over the whole of Europe and are the only species which are native to Great Britain.

Iris Lore

The iris has been known from the earliest times and it was probably the wide and brilliant range of its colours which first attracted attention and it became known as the 'Rainbow Flower'. It took its name from the Greek goddess, Iris, daughter of Taumas and the ocean nymph Electra, the personification of the rainbow and the messenger of the gods. She is generally represented as using the rainbow as her pathway through the sky and legend has it that when she visited the earth, under her footsteps rose the flowers that bear her name. To the Egyptians the Iris stood as a symbol of majesty and power. It was placed on the brow of the sphinx and on the sceptres of their kings, the three petals of the flower typifying faith, wisdom and valour. The Romans dedicated the iris to Juno, goddess of the moon. Four thousand years ago in Crete, the iris was the flower of prince and priest. It is widely held that the lilies referred to in the bible, 'even the lilies of the field' were in fact irises, identified as *I.pseudacorus*, since lilies are not native to the Holy Land, whereas the 'yellow flag' appears there in profusion. The confusion between the iris and the lily continued through the Middle Ages. Mrs Anley, in her lovely book on irises written in 1946, tells us that in the twelfth century an Arabian agriculturist wrote of the 'Violet Lily' when describing the culture of the iris. A little later an Arabian physician told of the many medicinal qualities of 'Irissia – the violet lily'. In France the Fleur-de-lis, used from 1180 as one of the badges of the kings of France, was invariably referred to as the 'Lily of France' but it was without doubt *I.pseudacorus*.

According to legend, King Chloris, at war with the Goths and hard pressed by his enemies, was directed to a safe crossing place over the River Lys by the profusion of yellow flags growing there and in gratitude adopted the flower as his personal device, calling it the 'Fleur-de-Lys'. Many years later Louis VII also chose the lovely water iris as his badge and it became known as 'Fleur-de-Louis'. Though there is an ongoing debate on this matter, we feel that we have a sound authority for holding that the fleur-de-lis is an iris since one of the earliest of our great botanists, Wylliam Turner in his *New Herball* of 1551, gives directions for the drying and storing of iris rhizomes under the heading 'of flour delice or fleur deluce'. John Parkinson in his *Paradisus* in 1629 also refers as an example to *I.variegata* as 'the yellow variable Flower de Luce'.

Figure 1.6
Stylised Forms of
the Iris as Used in
Heraldry

As to the name 'Fleur-de-lis' there are other derivations suggested apart from 'Fleur-de-Lys' and 'Fleur-de-Louis'. 'Fleur-de-lis' itself from the French word for a lily; fleur delice, flower of delight; fleur-de-lueur, fleur-de-lux, flower of light. Whichever may be right the iris fits perfectly all these names and meanings. As in its stylised form as the fleur-de-lis the iris was used heraldically through the ages, so in its more natural form the flower has appealed to artists from the earliest times. (Figure 1.6) With its elegant symmetrical form and its sympathetic colour combinations it has unsurpassed decorative value.

The oldest pictured iris appears in a fresco of the Priest King on the wall of the Palace of Minos at Knossos. It has long formed part of the iconography of painters in Europe, especially in Italy and Holland. Well-known examples of paintings in which irises appear are 'The Madonna of the Rocks' by Leonardo da Vinci, Dürer's 'Virgin and Child' and the 'Adorrazione' by Hugo van de Goes, which includes recognizably both *I.florentina* and *I.pallida*. In all these works the iris was used as a symbol of the birth of Christ. In the National Gallery of Victoria, Australia, there is a Flemish work of about 1500 which includes a beautifully drawn, almost botanical representation of what must be *I.trojana*. The iris was also seen in carvings in temples in India and in Asiatic palaces. In China and Japan stylised forms of *I.ensata* and *I.laevigata* have always featured in paintings, embroideries and lacquer work, being so well suited to the formal style of art of those countries.

Uses of the Iris

Again from the earliest times the iris has been known and valued for its many medicinal and economic uses. The Greeks and Romans used the dried rhizomes in perfumery as well as in medicine, and Macedonia and Corinthia were famous for ointments flavoured with irises. In the third century orris oil was numbered among the rare spices of the kings of Egypt.

The most widely used product of the iris is orris root, produced from the rhizomes of *I.florentina*, *I.pallida* and *I.germanica*, which are extensively grown for the purpose in northern Italy and known as giaggiolo. The rhizomes are dug up in August and trimmed, peeled and dried in the sun. For this purpose holes are pierced in each root and they are strung like beads and hung on lines like washing. When fresh the roots have a bitter aromatic flavour but after being dried, and stored for at least two years, they develop a distinct odour of violets. An early medicinal use of orris root was for the cure of scrofula and some diseases of the blood. Small beads of orris were inserted into the open wounds to keep them from healing too soon, orris being used because of its tendency to dilate in liquid.

Another article made from orris root was the dentarnolo, or finger, used as a teething ring for babies. Hard as a bone and complete with its own natural fluoride, it was invaluable in keeping the teeth white and the mouth healthy. Grains of the root, variously coloured, were used to throw on fires to give a pleasant smell, while tiny chips of the root were used for chewing to sweeten the breath. Rosary beads were also commonly made from the orris root. Fresh orris root, in granular form, was used for the treatment of bronchitis and diarrhoea and the juice of the root, bruised with wine, as a purge in cases of dropsy and for the removal of freckles. The essence of the root, oil of orris or orris camphor, has an intense odour of fresh violets and was widely used in perfumery.

It is in the form of orris powder that the root has been most extensively used. As an inhalant it was an effective treatment for complaints of the lung. Mixed with anise it was used as a perfume for linen (mentioned in the wardrobe accounts of Edward IV in 1480) and the powder was used to sweeten the rinsing water in laundries. It was used in curing tobacco, for scenting soap, tooth paste, shampoos and lotions, in face powder and in powder for wigs. Orris powder is still very much used in perfumery and for pot pourri. It is valuable not only for its own subtle and lasting fragrance, but as a natural fixative which has the power to enhance the odour of other ingredients. Large quantities of the roots are imported into this country from Tuscany and the Po valley where there is still a considerable home industry. The roots are also used in the making of Chianti. They are in this case steeped and the juices are added to the maturing wine to give it a very special flavour.

Orris flour or starch, a very finely ground powder, is also used for scenting snuff, in confectionery and for flavouring certain kinds of brandy. 'Iris Cake' can also be made and can still be bought in Florence, but rumour has it that it looks better than it tastes. Apart from orris root the most important economic product of the iris comes from *I.versicolor*. Native and widespread in eastern North America, it is grown extensively for commercial use in northern Italy. Its rhizome is known as 'Blue Flag Root' and is the source of Iridin or Irisin, a powdered extractive, bitter, nauseous and acrid with diuretic and aperient properties. It is used in medicinal preparations for the purification of the blood and considerable quantities are imported into this country from northern Italy and Trieste.

From the leaves of *I.florentina* was produced Iris Green or verdiris, a colouring agent once popular with artists. The universal *I.pseudacorus* was also used in the past in a number of ways. The rhizome has similar medicinal properties to that of *I.versicolor*, acting as a powerful cathartic. The powdered root was used for sweetening linen and as a snuff and it was also an ingredient of an antidote for poison. The seeds when ripe and well roasted produced a beverage similar, and some said superior to coffee. The flowers produced a beautiful yellow dye and the roots, with sulphate of iron, a lasting black dye. The root is a powerful astringent and was used in tanning and in making ink. The leaves were also used for fodder.

There were a number of minor uses for the various species. The powdered root of *I.tectorum* was used by ladies in China for whitening their skin. This is the lovely flower which was grown on the thatched roofs of houses in Japan and took its name from 'tectum', the Latin word for roof. From *I.sibirica* was obtained a powerful drug with emetic and laxative properties. The root of *I.lactea* was used externally to relieve rheumatic pains, while a distillation of the root and leaves was effective in reducing fever. Finally, the strong leaves of *I.spuria* were, and still are occasionally, used in Mediterranean countries in basketwork.

The History of the Genus

We have seen that irises were known from very early times and illustrations exist which are thousands of years old. They were clearly valued through the ages for their beauty and decorative quality but, for many centuries, were grown chiefly for their various and valuable medicinal uses. There are a number of references in the works of Theophastus, the Greek philosopher, of about 300 BC, and in the writings of Pliny in the first century AD. Irises were described by Dioscorides in his *Materia Medica* (AD 50) being considered not at all as garden plants but as a source of drugs. Similarly, in the *New Herball* of Wylliam Turner, published in London in 1551, the emphasis is on the medicinal use of the plants. Later in the sixteenth century we have a hint of irises being appreciated as flowers when John Gerard described them in the list of plants in his garden. But here again we suspect that they were grown at least partly for their medicinal value since Gerard was a surgeon and herballist as well as one of the first professional gardeners. However, it is known that their decorative value in gardens must have already been appreciated since Dykes refers to the fact that the lovely white *I.albicans* became naturalised in various parts of Europe because the Mohammedans carried it with them on their campaigns and used it as a decoration in their graveyards. It was, however, Carolus Clusius, the Flemish botanist, who first showed an intimate knowledge of, and interest in, irises solely as flowering plants. This was only a little later than Gerard, since, between 1576 and 1601, Clusius published various accounts of rare plants he had observed in his travels around Europe. He described in detail a dozen or so iris species under some unfamiliar names but we can recognise among them such basic species as *I.xiphium*, *I.pumila*, *I.spuria*, *I.sibirica*, *I.aphylla* and *I.variegata*.

The number of known species increased but slowly and in the Linnaean Herbarium, dating from the eighteenth century, 24 species were included but this number was soon increased by the results of Pallas' journey in Northern Asia, described in 1773. From then on the story of the genus as a whole is one of the discovery, identification and naming of new species, the development of hybrids by accident or design, and attempts at classification. The earliest of these, after Linnaeus (1753), was in 1863 by the German, Alefeld, but as he used a different basis of diagnosis for each of his groups the confused result did not meet with much approval. He was followed by another German, Klatt of Hamburg, whose classification was based mainly on the characteristics of capsules. This brought together in the same groups some strange bedfellows and was quite unsatisfactory.

The confusion about irises which existed at this period can be illustrated by the fact that in the famous *Botanical Magazine* between 1787 and 1904 there were published descriptions and illustrations of 280 irises, thought to be separate species and of these, only some 80 or 90 would be acknowledged as such today. Incidentally, it is a matter of pride to the irisarian that when William Curtis published the first of the series of the *Botanical Magazine* he chose for the subject the lovely iris *I.persica*. The confusion was slightly lessened when in 1892 J.G. Baker, Keeper of the Herbarium at Kew, published the most authoritative work so far, *The Handbook of the Irideae*. This was a thorough, scientific account of all the then known species but was based largely on herbarium study and designed for the botanist. The information it contained was put into more popular form for the gardener by the Curator of the Cambridge Botanical Gardens, R. Irwin Lynch, in his splendid work *The Book of the Iris* in 1904. Apart from detailed descriptions and cultivation notes, this work included a simple and logical classification based on rootstocks and was a turning point of the development of knowledge of the genus. It was dedicated to the great man of the iris, Sir Michael Foster, and it was he who, rather earlier, had done so much to stimulate interest in irises. He was Professor of Physiology at Cambridge University and his hobby was gardening with a special interest in irises. In the lovely garden of his house 'Ninewalls', built on a chalk hill at Shelford near Cambridge, he was one of the first to demonstrate the value of irises as garden plants. He collected and grew all the species he could; he sponsored a number of plant-collecting expeditions; he was reponsible for the identification and introduction of a number of new species and is rightly regarded as the founder of the cult of the iris in this country. He himself produced a monograph on bulbous irises and was working on a study of the whole genus at the time of his death. It was he who inspired Dykes to take over this task. W.R. Dykes was a master at Charterhouse School and, although he had no previous interest in gardening, his contact with Foster developed in him a passion for irises to which he devoted the rest of his life. In his two gardens at Godalming he grew every kind of iris he could obtain and in a few years he became the world authority. He introduced and named a number of new species and in 1913 published the monumental work *The Genus Iris*. In this work he described every species in the fullest detail on the basis of his observations of the living plants rather than simply of herbarium material. The beautiful drawings by F.H. Round were made from flowers taken from Dykes's garden. The book has remained the standard work on the genus and can be said to have put irises firmly on the horticultural map.

Since then there has been a steady expansion of knowledge of irises as more species are discovered and identified and as more studies are made of the flora of remote areas. The application of scientific techniques to botanic investigation has led to various modifications in the accepted Dykes classification, but so far no one has attempted a complete taxonomic study of the genus. Pending this, the American Iris Society has adopted the classification devised by G.H.M. Lawrence while Sidney Linnegar's version (Appendix VI) is offered in the hope that it may prove useful to gardeners.

Scientific developments in hybridising have led to some remarkable changes, not only with regard to bearded irises, as will be told later, but also with regard to some of the species. As an example, by the use of colchicine, tetraploid Siberian irises have been produced which are twice the size of the normal and bear flowers 6 inches across of great substance and with flaring falls. They are virtually a man-created species, and in an age of test-tube babies who knows what will happen next?

Perhaps more important than these scientific developments has been the steady expansion of interest all over the world in the growing of iris species. It is wonderful to know that they are now grown and loved in many countries to which they were never native, such as Australia, New Zealand, South Africa and South America.

The Tall
Bearded Iris

In this brief historical account of the genus as a whole we have made no mention of the development of the tall bearded iris, for this is a dramatic and romantic story which deserves to be treated on its own. It begins way back in history, certainly 350 years ago, when it

24

is known that there were many wild types of bearded iris in a wide range of colours and patterns. These were thought to be separate species and were given group names such as amoena, neglecta, plicata and squalens. They were, however, and this was finally established by Dykes, natural hybrids of the two important species from which the whole range of TBs sprang − *I.pallida* and *I.variegata*. *I.pallida* is native to Northern Italy, has bluish-lavender flowers and stems about 60-90 cm (2-3 ft) high. *I.variegata* comes from the Balkans and has yellow standards and brown falls with heavy veining and stems only 40-45 cm (16-18 ins) in height. Growing together wild and in gardens they gave rise to many seedlings almost infinitely varied in colour and pattern.

In the early years of the nineteenth century a number of these were described for the first time and given Latin names by von Berg of Neuenkirchen. In about 1822 de Bure, of Paris, introduced the first garden variety of bearded iris into commerce. It was a plicata, which with becoming modesty he named after himself 'Buriensis'. So it was this man who set in train the sequence of events which led to the development of the vast range of wonderful varieties now available. He influenced an eminent French horticulturist, M. Jacques, to grow and sell iris seedlings and give them publicity. He in turn inspired a French nurseryman, M. Lemon, to specialize in irises and he included many of these in his widely distributed catalogues. Of the hundreds of varieties he introduced the finest were probably 'Jacquesiana', named for the man who inspired his work and possibly raised by him, and 'Mme Chereau', a tall mauve and white plicata which can still be seen at Kew. Lists of his irises appeared in the catalogues of other nurserymen, notably the Verdiers of Paris, Van Houtte of Ghent and John Salter of London. All of these also offered seedlings of their own, and in the 1870s and 1880s a number of nurserymen such as Robert Parker, Thomas Ware and especially Peter Barr, were raising and introducing new varieties on a regular basis. We do not know if they made hand crosses or relied on the bees, but they tried to be selective and certainly produced a wide variety of colour forms. But no marked advance was brought about in growth characteristics or in obtaining larger flowers or greater substance. The famous 'Gracchus' raised by Ware which gained First Class Certificate in 1885 can still be seen and seems a pathetically poor thing. It seemed that no improvement was possible, but all that was changed by the discovery and introduction from the Near East between 1885 and 1889 of the large flowered species, *I.trojana*, *I.cypriana* and *I.mesopotamica* and varieties of these such as 'Ricardi' and 'Amas'. Although the hybridisers of the time were unaware of this, these species were in fact tetraploids and the spectacular improvement they brought about was due to the difference between their chromosome count and that of the older species, which were diploids. It was found that by crossing them with *I.pallida* and other diploids there would occasionally appear a fertile tetraploid with large flowers, improved form and substance and great vigour which could be used for further breeding. It was Sir Michael Foster who introduced the new species and he was the first to use *I.cypriana* and *I.mesopotamica* in his crosses, with magical results, for among many other seedlings he produced 'Caterina', 'Lady Foster' and later 'Kashmir White', ancestors of a long line of notable varieties. The famous French raisers, Vilmorin, Andrieux et Cie produced in 1904 the splendid 'Oriflamme' and later, in 1910, the sensational 'Alcazar', a huge bitone of tremendous vigour and substance widely used for breeding. In the pre-war years other raisers followed on from Foster using the tetraploid species as parents: in Germany, Goos & Koenemann; in France, Cayeux et le Clerc, Millet and Denis and in England Sir Arthur Hort and Amos Perry, all producing remarkable varieties. Then came yet another breakthrough when in 1917 A.J. Bliss, a retired engineer living in Devon, introduced a rich purple iris with velvety falls which was something new and sensational. This was the famous 'Dominion' which had immense influence on the future. It was raised from one of Foster's clones 'Amas', crossed with a hybrid of *I.pallida* and *I.variegata* and the lustrous texture of the falls was a revelation. From this iris came a series of magnificent varieties — the Dominion strain — among which were 'Cardinal' and 'Bruno', widely used for breeding. These irises were introduced into commerce by Robert Wallace and when they were first shown at a dinner in London, M. Mottet, Chef de Culture of Vilmorin et Cie, was moved to declare with splendid fervour that they were the finest irises in all the world.

In America the pattern of iris development followed closely that of Europe. The original settlers certainly took with them to the New World the range of then known species, and by the early nineteenth century the familiar forms such as germanica, florentina etc. were grown and known generally as 'Flags'. Towards the end of the century the first great American hybridiser, Bertrand H. Farr, imported from England the entire collection of Peter Barr's irises and established a nursery at Wyomissing. He began raising his own seedlings using the tetraploid species and with great success. Among his many seedlings perhaps 'Quaker Lady' was outstanding and remained a favourite on both sides of the Atlantic for many years. He marketed not only his own seedlings but a wide range of the best varieties from European raisers and brought to American gardeners the revelation of the glory of the new race of TBs. In the pre-war period there were a number of important breeders in America.

Grace Sturtevant set out to produce a really good yellow and suc-
ceeded with the famous 'Shekinah'. Bruce Williamson of Indiana
raised the great 'Lent A. Williamson', a bitone with blue standards
and rich purple falls, spoken of as the American 'Dominion'. In
Nebraska the Sass brothers, Hans and Jacob, developed a series of
remarkable hybrids including the well-known 'King Tut' and
'Rameses' from which derived many of the later pink varieties.
William Mohr, of California, using the tetraploid species produced
a series of varieties in a medley of colours including the pale blue
'Conquistador' and the red-violet 'Esplendido'. His work was continued by Sydney B. Mitchell, one of the greatest of all hybridisers,
whose wonderful array of successes culminated in the truly magnificent yellow 'Alta California'.

Back in England W.R. Dykes, having completed his study of the
whole genus, had turned to hybridising and produced many
hundreds of seedlings. Among the best of these were 'Amber', a
pale yellow, 'Moonlight', a yellowish-white and 'Wedgewood', a
medium blue. But his most famous seedling was 'W.R. Dykes' which
he saw in flower once only in the summer before his death in 1925
and which was named for him by his wife in the following year. It
was a magnificent yellow self, the first true yellow produced, and
was sold by the Orpington Nurseries at the staggering price of £20.
It created a world-wide sensation and was used for breeding for
many years. Mrs Dykes continued her husband's work and her
'Gudrun' was an outstanding white.

In the post-war period the European scene was dominated by
French raisers. Vilmorin followed their triumph with 'Alcazar'
with the even more resplendent 'Ambassadeur', a vigorous red-
brown bitone with a velvety texture, and the violet blend 'Dejazet'
and many others. M. Denis raised a series of ricardi-based seedlings
including the famous 'Mlle Schwartz'. Millet et fils also used ricardi
for a line of fine bitones ending with 'Germaine Perthuis'. Ferdinand
Cayeux then took over with a fabulous range which won for him
ten Dykes Medals in ten years with such masterpieces as 'Jean
Cayeux', 'Pluie d'or' and 'Deputé Nomblot', still flowering well
at Kew.

In England Amos Perry continued his introductions; Mrs Murrell
gained fame with the grey-white 'White City'; Sir Arthur Hort raised
such beauties as 'Leonato' and 'Ann Page' while G.L. Pilkington
produced many fine varieties culminating in 'Sahara', golden winner
of the Dykes Medal in 1935.

In later years in England fine irises were raised by a number of
enthusiastic amateurs such as Harry Randall, Canon Benbow, Sir
Cedric Morris, H. Castle Fletcher and H. Senior Fothergill. In New
Zealand Mrs Jean Stevens did great work on amoenas and her

27

'Pinnacle', with white standards and yellow falls, broke new ground in the 1940s. But it was in the USA that the great explosion of iris breeding took place and thousands of new varieties have been introduced over the years, and huge nurseries such as Schreiner's offer hundreds of wonderful irises in their annual catalogues. Of the many famous American raisers only a few can be mentioned such as Paul Cook, Edward Essig, Carl Salbach, Dr Kirkland, Dr Kleinsorge, Dr Randolph, Robert Schreiner and Orville Fay. There are many others, of course, and from their efforts we now have a range of the most beautiful tall irises in a profusion of colours, forms and patterns, amazingly derived from the unpromising basis of those two species from Central Europe.

Intermediates and Medians

The story of the intermediate iris takes us back again to Sir Michael Foster. It was he who first suggested to W.J. Caparne, an artist and iris-lover living in the Channel Islands, that he should force some tall bearded irises in his greenhouse so that they would flower early and he could put their pollen on the early flowering dwarfs in the open garden. This he did with some success and produced a range of smaller, early-flowering bearded irises which came between the species dwarfs and the TBs. In Germany Goos & Koenemann were working on the same lines and produced a list of their own. In America the Sass brothers followed suit and, using the tetraploid TB species, raised vastly improved forms such as 'Autumn Queen' and the lovely yellow 'Golden Bow'. Since then intermediates have been developed in the same way as the TBs in a wide range of colours and forms with some outstanding varieties such as 'Small Ripples' and 'Lemon Flurry'.

The form of dwarf originally used was *I.chamaeiris* but it was then found that *I.pumila* would give better results. In the early 1940s Paul Cook, working with Geddes Douglas, crossed *I.pumila* with tall bearded irises from Tennessee and the result was an entirely new hybrid, neither miniature nor intermediate, but flowering between the two, vigorous, floriferous and fertile, with branched stems and flowers in perfect proportion. The first of these came from Cook in 1951, the now famous quartet — 'Green Spot', 'Fairy Flax', 'Baria' and 'Brite'. Then in 1953 Douglas introduced among others the lovely pale blues 'Small Wonder' and 'Tinkerbell'. Since then a vast range of varieties of infinite colour combinations has become available. Aptly named at first 'Lilliputs' these little beauties are now officially called SDBs and they form a most valuable addition to any garden. They represent yet another triumphant breakthrough in the development of the iris.

CHAPTER 2

Bearded Irises in Bed and Border

In this and the following chapters up to Chapter 8, we shall be dealing with the different types of iris, showing how they can be used in various parts of the garden and discussing their care and cultivation. Before doing so we thought it would be fun to show a layout for an ideal garden for the real iris enthusiast. This provides space for all the sections and would make a splendid feature in that 'stately home' garden which we all dream about.

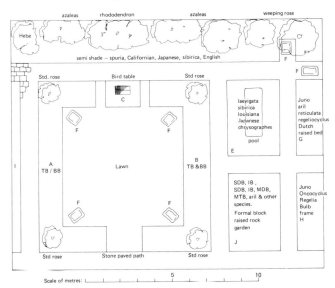

Figure 2.1
An Iris Garden
for the
Enthusiast
(Plan 1)

Beds A and B	Tall bearded and border bearded irises — see Chapter 2.
Bed C	Miniature tall bearded irises underplanting a thatched bird table.
Bed D	Lime-hating, semi-shady irises and spuria and Californian — see Chapter 4.
Bed E	Formal pool for *sibirica*, Louisiana and Japanese irises — see Chapter 5.
Beds F	Stone sinks for miniature dwarf bearded and *I.cristata* — see Chapter 6.
Bed G	Sheltered raised bed for Junos etc. See Chapter 7.
Bed H	Bulb frame for Juno and other tender irises — see Chapter 7.
Bed I	Border for cut flowers — Dutch, Californian, unguicularis — see Chapter 8.
Bed J	Formal rock garden for dwarf irises.

29

As a result of the dramatic developments in bearded irises described in the last chapter there is now available a fabulous range of flowers which must come as a revelation to those who still think of irises as 'blue flags'. First as to colour — there are the irises of one colour, known as 'selfs' ranging right through the rainbow from white to black, with dark, light and pastel shades of each tint. Then there are the amoenas, which have white or near-white standards and coloured falls, the neglectas with light-blue standards and purple-toned falls, and the plicatas, with light background overlaid with veining, dotting and stitching of a darker colour. Nowadays there are infinite variations of these basic themes with every sort of colour combination and with often brilliantly coloured and contrasting beards. In form and size, too, the bearded irises have changed almost beyond recognition and it is a far cry from the old drooping falls and floppy standards to the wide, flaring and ruffled falls and domed standards of the modern TB.

Although suited to many applications in the garden, the bearded irises are seen at their dramatic and dazzling best when massed together in formal beds or borders. Here the range of colours can be seen to advantage, use can be made of variations in height to produce a graded effect and of the differences in flowering times to give a long flowering period. There are few opportunities for the ordinary gardener to achieve the magnificent effect of the massive plantings such as were formerly to be seen in Kew Gardens, where huge beds, arranged in a setting of wide lawns, presented a dazzling summer spectacle. None the less, in a smaller formal or semi-formal garden, with paths of stone the effect can be almost as magnificent. For such an arrangement we would use together the three later flowering groups, tall bearded, border bearded and miniature tall bearded which can all be planted at the same time and dealt with together at each stage of their development. With them, to give variety of scale and to extend the flowering period, the smaller types, MDB and SDB can be introduced as they require the same general cultivation.

Cultivation

Bearded irises are most amenable plants but they do demand two conditions if they are to grow and flower well. First, they must be planted in a sunny position. If planted in the shade they will certainly grow and produce leaves but they are not likely to flower well, if at all, since the rhizomes need to be baked in the sun during the summer months. Secondly, they require good drainage so that the fleshy roots will remain sweet and healthy and the rhizomes will be kept free from rot. Waterlogged ground is the arch enemy of the bearded iris. In light soils this will present no problem but in heavy clay soil it may be necessary to dig deeply and incorporate fibrous compost to keep the subsoil open and it may well be desirable to raise the level of the beds by 5-8 cm (2-3 ins).

Soil and Soil Preparation

The ideal soil is a rich, sandy loam which can be slightly acid or slightly alkaline, in the range pH 6 to 7.5. It should be clean, of course, and if it is in good heart the only preparation needed is digging thoroughly to two spades' depth and the incorporation of bone meal. If it is in poor condition then organic, humus-forming materials should be dug in such as leaf mould, peat, hop manure, spent hops or properly made garden compost. Fresh animal manure should not be used. If the soil is heavy clay, then, as suggested above, more drastic measures must be taken. The soil must be broken down by thorough deep digging and the incorporation of rough compost such as old mushroom compost, which is specially good since it contains lime in the form of magnesium limestone. During preparation organic fertilisers such as hoof and horn and dried blood in small quantities can be forked in and thoroughly mixed with the soil, together with superphosphate of lime and sulphate of potash.

Although bearded irises can be grown on nearly pure chalk, a heavily limed soil is not really desirable and if lime is required to neutralise excessive acid it should be given in the form of magnesium limestone or dolomite chalk.

When to plant

Bearded irises can be planted, or divided and replanted, at any time between mid-summer and spring, but it must be remembered that the later in this period that they are put in the less chance there is of flowers for the next season. The best time is about 5-6 weeks after flowering is over, so for tall bearded irises in the United Kingdom that would be about the beginning of August. At this point in its life cycle the plant will have developed quite substantial roots on the rhizomes for the next year and will be entering a period of semi-dormancy. The roots will be strong enough to anchor the rhizome firmly to the ground and there will be time for the plant to get well established before the winter sets in. Transplanting in the same garden can be done immediately after flowering, but in this event care must be taken not to damage the new roots which will be less well developed and to firm the plants well into the ground to prevent wind rock.

How to plant

In formal iris beds or borders the plants are best arranged in groups of 3, 5 or 7 of one variety, with 30 cm (12 ins) between the plants and 50 cm (20 ins) between the groups. In less formal settings the plants may be arranged in rough circles each of one variety. These arrangements make it easier to keep track of where the different irises are when they develop into large clumps, as they will surely do, and will facilitate further division and replanting.

Figure 2.2
Setting out
of Rhizomes

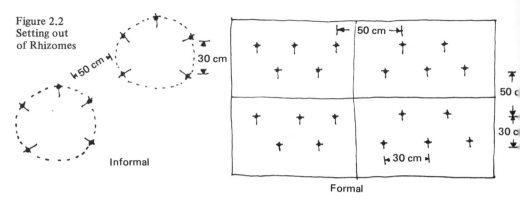

Informal

Formal

Figure 2.3
Diagram showing
Depth of Planting
(note soil level)

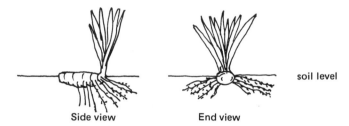

Side view   End view   soil level

For each plant a hole should be made large enough to take the whole root system and a ridge formed in the middle. The roots should be divided and spread out each side of the ridge and well firmed in so that the rhizome sits on the ridge in the middle. Nurserymen sometimes shorten the roots to 10 cm (4 ins) or so and the ideal practice described may not be possible. In this case the roots may be firmed into a single hole without much harm. In heavy soil the rhizome should have its upper surface clear of the soil level. In light soil the rhizomes may be 5-10 cm (2-4 ins) below the surface and this will make it easier to plant them firmly. They will rise to the surface themselves in due time so that the tops of the rhizomes are exposed to the sun. A few weeks after planting it is a good idea to examine the beds and firm in any plants which may have become loosened. Before planting the fans of leaves should be cut down to about 20 cm (8 ins) to prevent wind rock.

Care and Cultivation

As far as cultivation goes bearded irises are not at all demanding but they appreciate and will reward proper care. The beds should be kept free of weeds and this can best be done by the careful use of chemical germination inhibitors containing simazine such as Weedex, Herbon Blue or Herbon Yellow. The latter, being in liquid form, is probably the easiest to use. Hoeing around irises must be done with the greatest care to avoid damaging the offshoots from the rhizomes and the shallow-growing roots. If weeds do get established the only answer is hand weeding, and in a well-established clump this can be very hard going, so it is worth while getting the beds really clean at the outset.

Top dressings should be applied in spring time and in the autumn. For the spring dressing the following mixture is recommended, applied at the rate of 60 grams per sq. metre (about 2oz per sq.yd) and lightly forked in:

Bone meal	4	
Superphosphate of lime	2	parts by weight
Sulphate of potash	1	
Sulphate of ammonia	1	

For the autumn dressing the same mixture is suitable but without the sulphate of ammonia. For these dressings compound fertilisers such as Growmore or Maxicrop can be used, but care should be taken to see that they have a low nitrogen content. Overfeeding with nitrogen will cause the plants to make too much leaf and inhibit flowering. So look at the numbers on the packet showing the ratio of NPK (nitrogen, phosphorus, potassium) and if the first number is low then the product will be suitable. Light dressings of superphosphate of lime immediately after flowering are also beneficial.

When the flowers are over the stems should be bent over and snapped off close to the rhizomes so as not to leave a short stem in which moisture can collect as this may lead to rot. During the summer and autumn the dead leaves should be removed from time to time by gently pulling sideways to keep the beds clean. In the late autumn the fans of leaves, which will by then have gone brown at the tops, can be cut down neatly to a height of about 20 cm. This will not only give a tidy effect, but will help keep the beds clean and allow the rhizomes to get the benefit of any sun there may be.

Watering

Although bearded irises sustain drought conditions fairly well, they appreciate an occasional watering in dry, hot summer weather. This is particularly desirable on light soils in long, dry spells. Irises should be watered-in after planting and a good tip is to flood the base of the plants just as they are coming into flower.

Propagation

New varieties of irises are produced by growing from seed, but the normal method of propagation is by the division of the rhizomes. Most bearded irises reproduce themselves with great vigour and it will be helpful to understand the way in which they do it. As supplied by the nurseryman the plant will consist of a single rhizome with a fan of leaves cut down to 20 cm (8 ins) or an old rhizome with two offshoots with similar fans of leaves. By flowering time each rhizome will have produced two or more offshoots ready for the following year and the increase continues in geometrical progression as illustrated in Figure 2.4. After three or four years the rhizomes in the clump will have become somewhat crowded and will climb over each other and become all tangled up. Before this happens, usually in the third year, the clumps should be lifted and divided. This should be done at the best planting time. Normally only the outside rhizomes should be retained and if only a few of the variety are required then the largest should be selected. When a new variety is required in great numbers then all the rhizomes can be replanted and even the old rhizomes can be put in again at a depth of 5 cm

Figure 2.4
Diagram showing
how the Iris
Increases in Growth

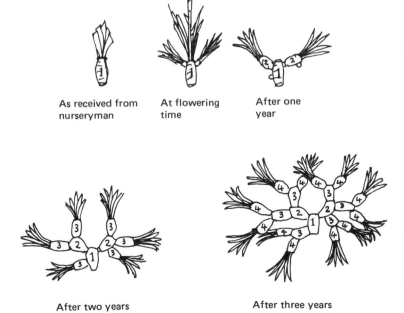

As received from   At flowering   After one
nurseryman   time   year

After two years   After three years

34

(2 ins) and may well produce plants which will flower in the second year. Individual 'eyes' can also be potted up in John Innes potting compost No. 2 and grown on in a cold frame. If the replanting is carried out in the dormant period the rhizomes can be left out of the ground for several weeks without harm, but before planting they should be soaked for several hours (preferably with a pinch of potassium permanganate dissolved in the water).

As a final cultivation hint it surely cannot do any harm to talk to your irises from time to time!

The two main diseases of the bearded iris are Rhizome Rot and Scorch.   Diseases

Rhizome Rot

This usually develops in the spring and is caused by a bacterial infection encouraged by waterlogged conditions. The leaves tend to yellow and parts of the rhizome become soft, mushy and very smelly. The rot usually occurs at the base of the old flowering stem, especially if a snag was left in the previous year. The treatment is to cut away the diseased part of the rhizome back to firm white flesh and dust the exposed part with potassium permanganate or other fungicide. The plant will normally suffer no ill consequences if treated in good time.

Scorch

This is a very different matter. The symptoms are that the leaves quite suddenly turn a vivid red-brown, as if on fire; the rhizomes remain firm but the roots wither away. The cause is unknown, but it seems that irises grown in very chalky soil are the most susceptible. The disease can occur at any time during the growing season and appears not to be contagious. There is really no treatment and the only thing to do is to lift the plant at once and burn it. If the variety is very special indeed it may be worth while to replant it in a very well drained bed in a greenhouse at least 15 cm (6 ins) deep, and there is an outside chance that it may recover and flower in a few years' time.

There are a few minor ailments such as leaf spot and bacterial leaf blight which are comparatively rare and are not serious. The best preventive measure is to make sure that dead leaves are removed regularly especially in wet weather and to keep the beds clean. Greenfly sometimes enjoy the tips of opening buds and should be controlled as soon as they appear. (Full details of pests and diseases are given in Appendix IV).

The Iris Garden

In planning an iris garden consideration must be given to the colour range, the height of the various types and to their varying flowering times. One of the great joys of bearded irises is that their colouring is such that they can be set out in almost any arrangement without disharmony. It is an odd thing, but they never seem actually to clash. However, we do suggest that some grouping of tones is desirable and that the darker and brighter-coloured varieties should be grouped farthest away from the house or the normal viewpoint. In general terms the grouping could be as follows:

very pale blue, soft pink, apricot, cream, soft bitones
tan, copper, lemon, mid-blue and blends
deep blue, golden yellow, red, black, white and contrasting bitones

with the last group farthest from the eye.

To illustrate the principles we offer two alternative layouts for an iris border. Plan 2A (Figure 2.5) using tall and border bearded

Figure 2.5
A Border of Tall Bearded and Border Bearded Irises Flowering at the Same Time in a Warm and Fairly Sheltered Position (Plan 2A)
V indicates the viewpoint.

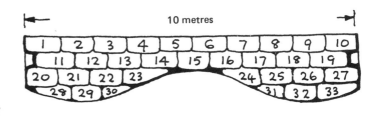

1 TB 'Blue Sapphire' white blue	18 TB 'Missouri' dark blue
2 TB 'Primrose Drift' pale yellow	19 TB 'Blue-eyed Brunette' brown
3 TB 'White City' blue white	20 TB 'Golden Forest' gold and white
4 TB 'Shepherd's Delight' pink	21 TB 'Patterdale' pale blue
5 TB 'New Moon' lemon	22 TB 'Benton Cordelia' orchid pink
6 TB 'Shipshape' medium blue	23 TB 'Whole Cloth' pale blue and white
7 TB 'Tarn Hows' cedar	24 TB 'Allegiance' deep blue
8 TB 'Stepping Out' purple and white	25 TB 'Sable Night' black
9 TB 'Winter Olympics' white	26 TB 'Ola Kala' deep yellow
10 TB 'Kilt Lilt' red and yellow	27 TB 'Tyrian Robe' purple
11 TB 'Pink Taffeta' pink	28 BB 'Lace Valentine' yellowish pink
12 TB 'Seathwaite' pale blue	29 BB 'Junior Prom' blue white
13 TB 'Mary Randall' rose pink	30 BB 'Frenchi' orchid red
14 TB 'Argus Pheasant' brown	31 BB 'Jungle Shadows' grey
15 TB 'Golden Alps' yellow and white	32 BB 'Bride's Pearls' white and yellow
16 TB 'Constance West' deep mauve-blue	33 BB 'Bayadere' metallic brown
17 TB 'Wabash' purple and white	

36

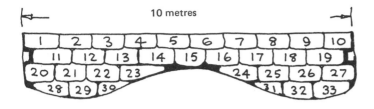

Figure 2.6
A Border with
Smaller Irises
Suitable for a Windy
Garden and giving a
Long Flowering
Period (Plan 2B)
V indicates the
viewpoint.

1 MTB	'Pee Wee' white	18 IB	'Piona' purple
2 BB	'Lace Valentine' pale pink	19 Aril	'Saletta' yellow and red
3 BB	'Junior Prom' blue white	20 SDB	'Widecombe Fair' white
4 BB	'Frenchi' orchid red	21 SDB	'Easter Holiday' yellow
5 BB	'Tulare' yellow	22 SDB	'Stockholm' cream
6 BB	'Molten Glass' orange	23 SDB	'Jane Taylor' pale blue
7 BB	'Bride's Pearls' white	24 SDB	'Gingerbread Man' brown
8 BB	'Bayadere' brown	25 SDB	'Cherry Garden' red
9 BB	'Jungle Shadows' grey	26 SDB	'Blue Denim' blue
10 MTB	'New Idea' violet purple	27 SDB	'Double Lament' purple
11 Aril	'Bethlehem Song' white/ yellow	28 MDB	'Knick Knack' white and lilac
12 IB	'Kiss Me Kate' blue white	29 MDB	'Atomic Blue' pale blue
13 IB	'Lemon Flurry' lemon	30 MDB	'Angel Eyes' blue and white
14 IB	'June Prom' blue	31 MDB	'Orchid Flare' violet
15 SDB	'Scintilla' ivory and gold	32 MDB	'Buttercup Charm' gold
16 IB	'Swizzle' brownish	33 MDB	'Black Baby' purple
17 IB	'Cotsgold' gold		

which will all flower at about the same time, and Plan 2B (Figure 2.6), with the smaller varieties suitable for an exposed, windy position and giving an extended flowering period. In Plan 3 (Figure 2.7) we show a semi-formal layout, mainly with bearded irises but incorporating some of the species to give variety and a longer flowering period.

In all the layouts suggested the named varieties are all ones which have won top awards either in the United Kingdom or the USA. They are included to show our ideas as to the blending of colours and if they are not available in commerce there will no doubt be more modern varieties of similar tones on the market. Those we have named have stood the test of time and can be relied upon to do well.

Figure 2.7
A Semi-formal
Mixed Iris Garden
(Plan 3)

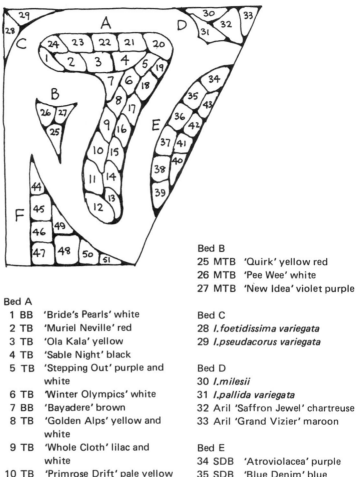

Bed B
25 MTB 'Quirk' yellow red
26 MTB 'Pee Wee' white
27 MTB 'New Idea' violet purple

Bed A
1 BB 'Bride's Pearls' white
2 TB 'Muriel Neville' red
3 TB 'Ola Kala' yellow
4 TB 'Sable Night' black
5 TB 'Stepping Out' purple and white
6 TB 'Winter Olympics' white
7 BB 'Bayadere' brown
8 TB 'Golden Alps' yellow and white
9 TB 'Whole Cloth' lilac and white
10 TB 'Primrose Drift' pale yellow
11 TB 'Blue Sapphire' pale silvery blue
12 BB 'Lace Valentine' pink
13 BB 'Junior Prom' lavender
14 TB 'Pink Taffeta' pink
15 TB 'Patterdale' pale blue
16 TB 'Rippling Waters' orchid blue
17 TB 'Argus Pheasant' brown
18 TB 'Golden Forest' yellow and white
19 TB 'Mary Todd' cedar
20 TB 'Missouri' deep blue
21 TB 'Amethyst Flame' deep mauve
22 TB 'Kilt Lilt' maroon and yellow
23 TB 'Allegiance' deep blue
24 TB 'Wabash' purple and white

Bed C
28 I.foetidissima variegata
29 I.pseudacorus variegata

Bed D
30 I.milesii
31 I.pallida variegata
32 Aril 'Saffron Jewel' chartreuse
33 Aril 'Grand Vizier' maroon

Bed E
34 SDB 'Atroviolacea' purple
35 SDB 'Blue Denim' blue
36 SDB 'Gingerbread Man' brown
37 SDB 'Cherry Garden' red
38 SDB 'Widecombe Fair' white
39 MDB 'Path of Gold' yellow
40 IB 'Piona' purple
41 IB 'Cotsgold' gold
42 IB 'June Prom' blue
43 SDB 'Scintilla' ivory and gold

Bed F
44 Californian 'No Name' yellow
45 Sibirica 'Cambridge Blue' blue
46 I.versicolor blue
47 Spuria 'Wadi Zem Zem' yellow
48 I.setosa, tall form, blue
49 Cal/sib 'Margot Holmes' wine
50 I.lactea
51 I.unguicularis

CHAPTER 3

Irises in the Mixed Border

For many years the common 'blue flag' — *I.germanica* — has been used as a feature in perennial borders in the traditional 'cottage garden'. Its hardiness and tough constitution have made it ideal to withstand the hurly-burly of such a situation. However, there are many other irises, equally robust, which will thrive in company with other perennials, and, because they come into bloom a little earlier than most, will add to the length of flowering time and extend the range of colour in the border.

In such situations it will not always be possible to provide the ideal growing conditions for irises, but most of them will not mind that too much. For example, most mixed borders are given a good supply of farmyard manure when being prepared (or they should be!), but for irises to flourish such treatment is acceptable only if the manure is very well rotted and deeply buried. Again, it may not be convenient to disturb a border to transplant bearded irises at the proper time, but this operation can be delayed until the late autumn without too much harm. And if early winter frosts then delay the operation still further into the spring, the irises will still survive quite happily, though some may lose a year's flowering.

Irises associate well with most flowers and when grown in a normal bed or border with asters, paeonies, delphiniums, phlox, papavers and other later-flowering plants they will help to provide colour all through the year. Their range of height allows them to occupy a variety of positions and the tremendous span of available colours and patterns makes it possible to include them with advantage in almost any colour scheme. The distinctive iris foliage, too, contrasts nicely with that of other plants and will normally remain attractive until well into the autumn.

For the back of the border or the centre of the island bed the tall kinds are obviously the best, and these would be the tall bearded and the spurias, the latter being especially useful since they flower rather later than the others — in late June and July.

Of the bearded irises there is a terrific range of choice both among the species and the thousands of named varieties. Dealing first with the species, one of the most useful is *I.pallida*, with handsome, grey-blue-green, almost evergreen leaves, delicate lavender-blue flowers and papery white spathes, ideal in the blue border and very floriferous. There is a specially fine form, *I.pallida dalmatica*, which has lovely pale-lavender flowers of good substance which are sweetly scented. There are also two very attractive variegated forms — *I.pallida variegata argentea*, which has green and white striped leaves overcast silver and is the commoner form and known sometimes as the 'zebra iris', and *I.pallida variegata aurea* with green and yellow striped leaves. Then there is a range of bearded species which can be planted appropriately to their height and colour and we list them in order of height. First, the handsome *I.cypriana*, one of the historic breeding irises introduced by Sir Michael Foster, pale lilac and reddish-purple and growing to 95 cm (3 ft 2 ins). It is not easy to obtain, but well worth searching for and very rewarding; then *I.germanica* itself, the common purple flag, still not to be despised as a garden plant providing brilliant patches of colour early in the season — 75 cm (2 ft 6 ins); *I.trojana*, another of the great historical species, pale blue and red purple with faint brown veining — 75 cm (2 ft 6 ins); *I.albertii*, a border bearded from Russia, a purple self which occasionally shows a form of crest — 60 cm (2 ft); *I.aphylla*, yet another historical species, known for centuries and well worth preserving, reddish-purple in two shades and growing to perhaps 45 cm (18 ins); *I.albicans* from Arabia, a lovely clear-white flower of pure form, very floriferous — about 35 cm (14 ins); *I.florentina*, the 'orris root' iris.

When it comes to choosing named varieties of bearded irises for the mixed border, the choice is so wide that it is really up to the individual to select for just the effect required. We can only suggest that it is as well to pick from among those which have been tried and not found wanting as garden plants. So we make no excuse for naming some of those which are truly great and completely reliable though they may not be among the recent fashionable introductions. As evidence of their quality they have all received the First Class Certificate of the Royal Horticultural Society. Going through the colour range we name:

'Cliffs of Dover', a fine white iris slightly ruffled and very free flowering

'White City', a famous old variety, pale grey-white also exceptionally free flowering

'Aurelian', a medium yellow with a small white blaze on the falls

'Gilston Gwyneth', a distinguished iris of pale grey-blue with a deeper centre flush

'Blue Rhythm', a tall and elegant mid-blue

'Jane Phillips', paler blue and very reliable

'Patterdale', pale blue and free flowering

'Blue-eyed Brunette', cigar brown with a blue spot on the falls, very striking

'Sable', as the name implies, a splendid purple/black

These are more or less self-coloured, selfs as they are called, but there are countless blends and bicolours such as, for example:

'Dancer's Veil', a superb white and violet plicata

'Stepping Out', another striking plicata, white with deep blue-violet edges

'Headlines', a bicolour with greyish white standards and velvety red-purple falls

There are, of course, many many more to suit all tastes, and among them mention should be made of the race known as aril-breds. Aril irises differ from other bearded irises basically because their seeds have a white aril or collar around one end. They comprise the four groups, regelia, oncocyclus, pseudo-regelia and psammiris which are native to the arid areas of eastern Europe and Asia. They are wildly exotic and spectacular in form and colour and in temperate climates require very special treatment in cultivation. From the earliest times hybridisers have been crossing arils with bearded irises in an attempt to transfer to the more easily grown groups the dazzling characteristics of the more difficult species. Most of the earlier results proved sterile but eventually William Mohr in California developed a superb strain which became known as 'Mohr' irises, among which the famous 'Elmohr' of rich mulberry colour and great substance was outstanding and is still strongly recommended. There are now very many arilbreds available and they are characterised by having flowers of rounded form with broad falls and domed standards and almost infinite variations in colour and pattern.

Also eminently suitable for the mixed border are the unusual irises known as 'remontants' or 'rebloomers'. These are irises which have two distinct periods of flowering, in the summer and the late autumn. Less robust usually than the normal irises, they are none the less very exciting to grow and add colour and interest late in the season. Interest in their development is increasing on both sides of the Atlantic and there are numerous varieties now available. Two beautiful and reliable varieties are 'Lovely Again' and 'Late Lilac'.

In the dwarf class we hesitate to select from the ever growing list of these lovely newcomers, but we do feel that the first of the lilliputs developed in America, 'Green Spot' — creamy-white with a green signal patch — and 'Small Wonder' — a fine mid-blue variety which is exceptionally vigorous — are 'musts' for the front of the border. The care and cultivation of these bearded irises have been dealt with in Chapter 2.

Among the beardless species perhaps the most useful in the mixed border are the Spurias, which deserve to be more generally known and more widely grown. They are the tallest of the irises and have handsome, sword-like leaves and when grown in clumps are very suitable for the back of the border or to act as sentinels at the ends. They flower later than other irises, from mid-June through July, and so extend the season of bloom. The flowers are similar to those of the bulbous Xiphiums but greater in diameter and with more slender and graceful petals. They come in shades of blue, yellow and white and yellow and there are hybrids in many colour combinations. Several flowers are produced on each stem, one above the other and close to the stem and the foliage is luxuriant and handsome. (The flowers are good for cutting and will last well if brought indoors just as they are about to open).

There are two groups of these irises, those which become dormant soon after flowering and those which retain their leaves right through to the winter. In the first group the three main species are *I.orientalis*, *I.crocea* and *I.monnieri*. *I.orientalis* (long known as ochroleuca) is an old favourite in cottage gardens. It has creamy-white flowers with a distinct yellow patch on the falls, sometimes described very aptly as 'butterfly blossoms'. It grows with great vigour and flowers prolifically at a height of 100 cm (3 ft 3 ins) or more. *I.crocea* (better known, and will be found listed, as *aurea*) has pure golden-yellow flowers similar in form to *I.orientalis* but without the patch and very slightly frilled. It flowers just a little later at about 100 cm. *I.monnieri* may well be a hybrid but is distinct in colour which is a pale lemon-yellow and in the smooth-textured flowers which are slightly shorter than the other two in the group.

In this group of summer dormants there are two very old hybrids, both raised by Sir Michael Foster, but outstanding and well worth growing. 'Monspur', said to be a cross between *I.monnieri* and *I.spuria*, is like *I.monnieri* but has striking clear cobalt flowers with a touch of gold and is still the best blue spuria. 'Shelford Giant' is unique and remarkable for the fact that it grows to a height of 180 cm (6 ft) no less. The flowers are large, lemon-white with a vivid yellow patch. The stems are very strong indeed, almost like steel, and will stand up to the severest gale without support. The plant is vigorous and reliable and looks most noble growing at the back of a wide border.

In the second group is the type plant, *I.spuria* itself, which has pale-blue flowers more slender than those of *I.orientalis* and is very free flowering, and a specially lovely form *I.halophila* with flowers of a delicate lilac-blue with a small gold patch. These are slightly shorter, about 75 cm (2 ft 6 ins). *I.demetrii* has deep violet-blue flowers and is quite tall, about 75 cm, and *I.klattii* is a shorter version, with the same colouring but with distinctly broader leaves. Finally, for the middle of the border there is the dwarf *spuria*, *I.kerneriana*, only some 25 cm (10 ins) high with soft yellow flowers. Many good spuria hybrids have been produced in the USA and among the earliest, and arguably still the best, are 'Wadi Zem Zem', a superb pure yellow and 'White Heron' a beautiful white form. Of later introductions 'Good Nature' is a larger and more magnificent version of the pure yellow *aurea* and 'Academus' is one of many attractive multi-coloured blends now available.

Spuria irises grow best in soil which is neutral to slightly alkaline and must be planted in full sun and have good drainage. The proper planting time is September and when planted the rhizome should be 5-10 cm below the ground and well firmed in. Spurias are heavy feeders and enjoy well-manured soil and regular fertilising. They sustain drought conditions quite well but will profit from an occasional watering especially before flowering. The non-dormant types prefer slightly moister conditions but will grow in any normal border. The dwarf *I.kerneriana* does not like lime. The spurias have longish thin rhizomes and the habit of the plants is to spread outwards and form a circle increasing in diameter year by year. They do not like to be disturbed and the clumps should be left as long as possible, even 10-15 years. If space is limited and the clumps have to be reduced, separate rhizomes can be detached and replanted in preference to lifting the whole clump. The summer-dormant types become untidy after flowering and can be cut down to the ground in August. The other type should be tidied up regularly by having the dried leaves cut off — not pulled off.

There are no serious diseases affecting spurias, but as they produce a lot of nectar they attract insects and are liable to be infested with aphids. So a watch should be kept for blackfly, which should be controlled by using derris or pyrethrum.

Other beardless irises which can profitably be used in a mixed bed or border are as follows:

I.lactea is the oriental plant variously known as *'ensata'* (of gardens), *'biglumis'* and *'pallasii'* but none of these names reflects the true beauty of this specially attractive plant. It has narrow leaves, pale blue-green in colour, which grow in a tight clump which spreads very slowly. They remain almost throughout the year, dying down only for a short period in mid-winter. The flowers are exquisitely elegant and unlike any other iris. They have narrow tapering falls, usually milky white with green and violet veins and stippling, giving almost a bird's egg effect. They flower at about 10-30 cm (4-12 ins) early in May and they tend to have their blooms down among the leaves giving a delicate sparkling appearance to the plant. *I.lactea* will grow in any soil if it takes to you. It stands drought conditions well and seems to require little attention apart from tidying up the dead leaves in winter and this should be done with care. It dislikes being disturbed or broken up and, if you are lucky, will form a fine clump which will remain for years getting better and better. New planting can be done from May to September.

Figure 3.1
Iris longipetala,
Iris delavayi and
Iris sibirica 'Cool Spring'

I.longipetala *I.delavayi* *I.sibirica* 'Cool Spring'

I.longipetala is an almost evergreen species native to the western states of North America. It grows easily in any sunny garden and has grey-green, almost grassy, leaves and delicate white and violet flowers with narrow petals, blossoming high among the leaves at about 60 cm (2 ft).

I.missouriensis, of which *longipetala* is probably a form, is similarly native to the western parts of the USA where it grows in profusion. It has white and lavender flowers, the falls having purple veining, is less tall — about 45 cm (18 ins) and is not evergreen.

These species flower in May and should be planted or divided in September. They require little attention and will make good, compact clumps which can be left for years. If they become too big then it is best to divide them into smaller clumps rather than into single rhizomes. This is advisable for all the fibrous-rooted species and the best way to do it is to use two forks, back to back, and prize apart the closely knit roots. These Americans naturally flourish in areas which have a moist spring and a dry summer, but they will do quite well in our normal climate. The flowers are held just above

44

the foliage and are delicate and graceful, an enhancement to any border.

I.setosa is an unusual and delightful species which will do well in the front of the border. Widely distributed from Japan across to Labrador and the eastern USA this plant looks like a miniature Japanese iris. The distinctive blue flowers have very short standards and a flat, three-petalled appearance. This is a moisture-loving iris but it will do well enough in normal soil if well watered. It dislikes lime. It flowers in June and the best planting time is September. Height about 20-30 cm (8-12 ins).

Finally, there are two lovely crested irises which are recommended.

I.milesii is a tall species with broad yellow-green ribbed leaves and flowers of pale reddish-purple with an orange crest, borne on branched stems at a height of 95 cm (3 ft 2 ins). It flowers in June and should be planted in July. Cultivation is more or less the same as for tall bearded irises.

I.tectorum is one of the really fine garden irises. This 'roof iris' from Japan has a special character of its own. The leaves are broad and yellow-green, tending to be a bit floppy but almost evergreen. The flowers are unusual in that the standards lie down almost level with the falls, and both being slightly frilly this gives an entrancing six-petalled lacy effect. They are a clear blue-lilac in colour with a distinct white beard. They flower at a height of about 35 cm (14 ins), are quite floriferous and will provide a dramatic drift of colour in June. There is a white form which is exceptionally beautiful but this is a rare bird and difficult to grow.

Figure 3.2
I.tectorum

Both these Evansias are easy to grow but *I.tectorium* has special cultural requirements. For some unknown reason it seems quickly to exhaust the soil so it likes to be moved to a new position as often as possible — at least every two years. This should be done in late June, just after flowering. It also tends to hoist its rhizomes out of the ground and expose the roots and a heavy mulch of well-rotted compost should be applied in the spring and autumn. All this you will find to be well worth while.

It should be noted that a number of the true moisture-loving irises can also be grown in a normal mixed border, but they will be less tall than when grown in their favourite boggy conditions. Among these are *I.sibirica*, *I.sanguinea*, our native *I.pseudacorus* and *I.versicolor*. In the border they will all benefit from a mulch of peat or compost to keep them from drying out in the summer. They will be described more fully in a later chapter.

Plan 4 (Figure 3.3) shows a suggested layout for a normal sunny mixed border, Plan 5 (Figure 3.4) a mixed dwarf border and Plan 6 (Figure 3.5) a mixed 'sword-leaf' border.

Figure 3.3
A Mixed Border
with Irises and
Other Plants
(Plan 4)

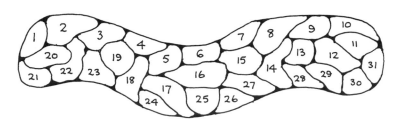

1	*I.pallida variegata*	17	Tradescantia 'Iris Prichard'
2	Aster 'Patricia Ballard'	18	Geranium 'Johnson's Blue'
3	Achillea 'Moonshine'	19	Paeonia 'Bowl of Beauty'
4	Iris 'Allegiance'	20	Eryngium 'Blue Dwarf'
5	Helenium 'Golden Youth'	21	Bergenia 'Sunningdale'
6	Phlox 'Iris'	22	Potentilla 'Gibson's Scarlet'
7	Armeria 'Bee's Ruby'	23	Polemonium 'Sapphire'
8	Hemerocallis 'Golden Chimes'	24	Iris 'Chiltern Gold'
9	Chry. 'Chobham Gold'	25	Erigeron 'Foester's Liebling'
10	*Centaurea steenbergii*	26	Iris 'Widecombe Fair'
11	*Iris milesii*	27	Aster 'Lady in Blue'
12	Rudbeckia 'Goldquelle'	28	Iris 'Ola Kala'
13	Paeonia 'Mme Furtado'	29	Geum 'Fire Opal'
14	Doronicum 'Spring Beauty'	30	Sedum 'Autumn Joy'
15	*Iris monnieri*	31	*Iris pseudacorus variegata*
16	Delphinium 'Blue Riband'		

Irises in the Mixed Border

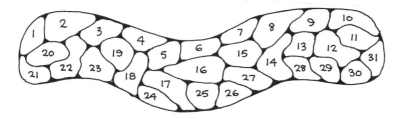

Figure 3.4
A Mixed Dwarf
Border with Irises
and Other Plants
(Plan 5)

1	Armeria 'Bee's Ruby'	16	*Iris pallida variegata*
2	Solidago 'Crown of Rays'	17	*Brunnera macrophylla*
3	Iris 'Austrian Sky'	18	Doronicum 'Spring Beauty'
4	Erigeron 'Foester's Liebling	19	Paeonia 'White Wings'
5	*Geum borisii*	20	Aquilegia 'Crimson Star'
6	*Geranium endressi* 'Wargrave'	21	Iris 'Widecombe Fair'
7	Potentilla 'Roulette'	22	Helenium 'Crimson Beauty'
8	*Campanula glomerata superba*	23	*Limonium latifolia* 'True Blue'
9	Iris 'Double Lament'	24	Coreopsis 'Goldfink'
10	Tradescantia 'Iris Prichard'	25	Iris 'Piona'
11	*Chrysanthemum rubellum* 'Clara Curtis'	26	Heuchera 'Red Spangles'
12	*Iris sibirica* 'Cambridge'	27	*Pulmonaria azure*
13	*Dictamnus fraxinella*	28	*Stachys lanata*
14	Aster 'Chatterbox'	29	Iris 'Chiltern Gold'
15	*Achillea taygeta*	30	Liatris 'Kobold'
		31	*Anchusa ceaspitosa*

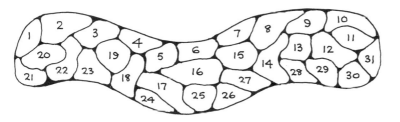

Figure 3.5
A Mixed 'Sword
Leaf' Border with
Irises and Other
Plants (Plan 6)

1	Hemerocallis 'Golden Chimes'	17	*Iris siberica* 'Cambridge'
2	Kniphofia 'Bee's Sunset'	18	Hemerocallis 'Stafford'
3	Gladiolus 'Green Woodpecker'	19	Paeonia 'Victoria'
4	Hemerocallis 'Ophir'	20	Iris 'Ola Kala'
5	Kniphofia 'Maid of Orleans'	21	Iris 'Widecombe Fair'
6	*Crocosmia masonorum*	22	*Hosta medio variegata*
7	Hemerocallis 'Delicate Splendour'	23	Tradescantia 'Iris Prichard'
8	Gladiolus 'Merry Widow'	24	*Hosta fortunea picta*
9	Kniphofia 'Sunningdale Yellow'	25	Hemerocallis 'Towhead'
10	Hemerocallis 'Royal Ruby'	26	Iris 'Piona'
11	*Lilium candidum*	27	*Iris lactea*
12	*Iris milesii*	28	Hemerocallis 'Pink Damask'
13	*Iris pallida variegata*	29	Iris 'Chiltern Gold'
14	*Iris sibirica* 'Anniversary'	30	Hemerocallis 'Francis Fay'
15	Iris 'Stepping Out'	31	Iris 'June Prom'
16	*Iris monnieri*		

47

CHAPTER 4

Irises in Wild or Woodland Gardens

Although bearded irises are best when planted in more or less formal situations and demand full sunlight, there are a number of the beardless types which flourish in wild surroundings and enjoy growing in varying degrees of shade. So for wild and woodland gardens there are some beautiful irises which will bring a special sparkle of colour and pattern to otherwise dull places at times when few other flowers are around.

For the grassy bank and for the small glade in the shrubbery, where the grass is cut back perhaps once or twice a year, there are the exquisite small bulbous irises of the Reticulata group. These come from the eastern Mediterranean and derive their name from the fact that the bulbs have a distinctive netted covering. They are suitable for growing in pans or in the rock garden but they are especially attractive in semi-wild surroundings. The flowers are normally blue-violet in colour, with a touch of gold on the falls, about 15-20 cm (8 ins) high, and the narrow foliage is short at flowering time but can increase to 60-70 cm (2 ft-2 ft 4 ins) after flowering is over. There are a number of species in the group and many named varieties, but for naturalizing it is probably best to stick to *I.reticulata* itself of which there are several lovely colour variations. The bulbs should be planted in the autumn, in groups and at a depth of 5-10 cm (2-4 ins), in good lightish soil without too much acid and in a well-drained position. The flowers will appear in the very early spring and for the following year the bulbs will develop offshoots which will provide drifts of these delightful flowers.

In the wilder open spaces of the garden where the grass is allowed to grow longer or in the small orchard among the fruit trees, splashes of colour and a touch of garden quality can be introduced by using irises of the Spuria group. These are handsome, strong-growing plants and when well established will hold their own in the grass and, as their foliage dies down quite quickly after flowering time, will not suffer from the occasional trimming of the grass. The best species for use in this application are the summer dormant types such as *I.orientalis* (commonly known as *ochroleuca*), the lemon-shaded *I.monnieri* and the deep golden *I.crocea*, better known as *I.aurea*. They can be planted singly or in groups as desired and will form handsome clumps which can be left undisturbed for years.

In similar wild situations the stronger forms of *I.sibirica* can be used with advantage to give a variation in colour and also *I.missouriensis* which thrives in really wild conditions. Plants of these species should be allowed to become well established before letting the grass grow into them but they can then be left alone for quite a time.

In semi-shaded positions, such as the edge of a deciduous shrubbery or in light woodland areas, sparkling colour effects can be obtained by the use of the bulbous English irises. These were originally known as *I.xiphiodes* and are descended from *I.latifolium*, native of the moist mountain meadows of the Pyrenees. Unlike their close relatives the Dutch and Spanish irises, they favour a dampish shady situation and neutral-to-acid soil. The bulbs should be planted in the autumn, 10 cm (4 ins) deep in groups 10 cm apart. The robust flowers are held on 50 cm (20 ins)-long, non-branching stems and come in a range of colours, blue, purple, white and white flecked with purple. They are good growers and will normally naturalise and look especially well against a dark leafy background.

Also very happy in a semi-shaded position is our well-known native *I.foetidissima*. This is one of the most interesting and adaptable of all the irises. It will do well almost anywhere and is about the only iris which will flower in really deep shade. In cultivation it will be found in all situations from the open allotment to the deepest wood. In the wild it can be seen in the Isle of Wight and around the Dorset coast, growing in wet, shady spots under the cliffs. It derives its unsavoury name from the fact that when the leaves are crushed they give off a pungent smell and this also explains its nicknames the 'stinking iris' and the 'roast beef plant'. Its old English name was 'gladdon', the origin of which is unknown, and it is frequently referred to as the 'Gladwin iris'. It has a wide distribution, spreading across Europe and Asia to China. It has broad, shiny, evergreen leaves and somewhat inconspicuous flowers which are rather like miniature Spurias with the standards bending outwards, giving a star-like effect, and are of a dull purplish-grey or creamy-brown colour. The flowers appear low in the foliage and often come out and fade unnoticed and it is not until the seed pods appear that it is realized that the plant has flowered at all. But the seed pods are the glory of the plant for in the autumn the capsules split open and display rows of brilliant scarlet seeds which remain attached throughout the winter and are dazzlingly attractive in their dark surroundings. They are much in demand for floral decoration to enhance the winter dried arrangements. There are several

Figure 4.1

English Iris

Seed Pods of
I.foetidissima

49

less common forms of this species, one having yellow flowers and another with white flowers and seeds. There is also a very fine variegated leaf form with green and gold striped foliage. These are all slow growers and like a good soil with plenty of humus and a little lime. The flowers appear in mid to late summer at a height of 37-45 cm (15-18 ins). They can be divided and replanted either in the spring or the autumn. The variegated form does not like to be moved about and once established should be left undisturbed.

Yet another iris which will be happy in a shady spot is *I.unguicularis*, the winter-flowering species from Algeria which does well almost anywhere provided the ground is dry. This is one of our real favourites and will be dealt with fully in Chapter 8.

In less wild woodland situations there are several iris species which will flourish in the semi-shade. We have in mind the shady glade with clearings between the larger shrubs where iris beds can be established which need not be completely weed free, but can be prevented from becoming overgrown by a good mulch of peat, leaf mould, or even sawdust or pine bark. In such beds one finds azaleas or similar shrubs and these can be beautifully enriched by underplanting with irises of the series Californicae, more usually known as Pacific Coast irises, or PCIs.

These are really splendid garden plants and deserve to be more widely grown. They are native to a strip of the west coast of the USA from Washington down to central California, and flourish in the wild on the western slopes of the Cascade and Sierra Nevada mountain ranges. They are closely related to Siberian irises and presumably in the dim past they came from eastern Russia by way of the Bering Strait. In this transition they evolved special characteristics which have made them among the prettiest of irises. The flowers are about the same size as those of the Siberians but crisper and less floppy. The falls are usually quite broad and more rounded and frilly and the standards are held at an angle and are slightly rippled. The colour range is wide — from cream, buff, yellow to lavender, purple, violet, blue to white. They are usually richly patterned with veins or patches of deeper shades of purple, maroon or red. In the countless wild hybrids there is a tremendous diversity of colours and patterns.

There is a considerable range of size, height and colour in the various distinct species which have been closely defined as follows:

I.bracteata, pale yellow, 15-20 cm (6-8 ins).
I.chrysophylla, cream, veined with gold or violet, 20 cm (8 ins).
I.douglasiana, purple, red, violet or white, 20-30 cm (8-12 ins). Evergreen.
I.fernaldii, pale creamy yellow, 20-30 cm. Evergreen.

I.hartwegii, cream, yellow or lavender, 20 cm.

I.macrosiphon, purple-blue, lilac, white & yellow, 25 cm (10 ins).

I.munzii, pale blue to purple, 50-60 cm (20-24 ins). Evergreen.

I.purdyi, cream, veined with purple or rose, 18-20 cm (7-8 ins). Evergreen.

I.tenax, deep purple shading through blue to white-yellow, 25-30 cm. Some forms are evergreen.

I.tenuissima, cream, veined purple or brown, 25 cm. Evergreen.

All these species will do well in semi-shaded positions but the remaining species in the group, *I.innominata*, has to have full sun and would be best planted at the edge of the glade. It is low growing and forms neat clumps with a multitude of flowers ranging in colour from the commonest golden-yellow form through lavender to purple, with the falls veined or netted with red-purple or brown lines.

Figure 4.2
Iris douglasiana

In addition to these species, which may not be all that easy to obtain, there are now many lovely named varieties, raised in the USA and this country, which are available on the market. In particular, Mrs Marjorie Brummitt has produced a series of 'Banbury' varieties which are quite magnificent — such as 'Banbury Beauty', 'Banbury Fair', 'Banbury Gem' and many more. These plants are all easy enough to grow and like good soil with considerable humus, slightly on the acid side, and they appreciate good drainage. They are all quite hardy, except possibly *I.munzii* which needs a little protection in winter. There are no pests or diseases to bother about except, of course, the inevitable slugs.

All the species will come true from seed and germinate readily and this is the best way to obtain these plants. The hybrids, however, will not come true from seed so their propagation has to be vegetative, by division. This has long been regarded as a hazardous operation but it can be done quite successfully with just a little care. The plants should be lifted about two months after flowering and divided into small clumps, making sure that each has some good strong roots. The rhizome and young roots should be wrapped in damp sphagnum moss which will keep the root-growth going. If they are then kept moist until planted all will be well.

You will find that some nurserymen are reluctant to send out actual plants of PCIs because of the possibility of their drying out in transit, but offer seed in a mixed variety. These should be sown in pots in the early autumn and the pots plunged in well-drained soil or ashes in an open situation. In the spring the seedlings should have developed four or five leaves and can be put individually into small pots in lime-free compost. Three months later they can be planted into their permanent positions. This is an exciting way of obtaining plants as one never knows what will happen and the variation in the colours and patterns of these haphazard hybrids is infinite and usually delightful. And, who knows, you may get an absolute winner.

Among the crested irises (Evansias) there are a number which like growing in the shade but they mainly need more attention than they would get in the semi-wild. There is, however, the charming species *I.gracilipes*, which will do well in a semi-shaded grassy location. It has most delicate and exquisite lilac flowers carried on wiry stems at about 20 cm (8 ins) and narrow arching foliage. It likes an acid soil and prefers a moist situation. The flowers appear in early summer and the time for replanting is the following early spring.

Another lovely dwarf species which enjoys the same conditions is *I.verna*. This is an early-flowering species which has blue-lilac flowers with orange markings on the falls. They are only 5-10 cm (2-4 ins) high and set in deep green, sword-like foliage. They give a charming crocus-like effect as they herald the coming of the spring.

Figure 4.3
Japanese Irises
(*I.ensata*)

Another important group of irises which should have place in the woodland clearing are the Japanese irises. These are all derived from the single species known as *I.kaempferi*, which is properly and botanically *I.ensata* and known to the Japanese as 'Hanashobu'. In its wild form it is little known nowadays and is not a very impressive plant, having rather ordinary red-purple flowers with small standards and large, oval floppy falls. From this simple species the Japanese have, over the years — indeed over the centuries — developed a range of large-flowered garden varieties, the feature of which is the virtual elimination of the standards as such and the enlargement of the falls. These flowers can be gigantic in size and spectacular in form and colour. Single blossoms may be as much as 30 cm (12 ins) in diameter. There are three main types — the so-called singles, with three broad, overlapping falls and tiny standards; doubles, which have six broad, overlapping petals, which are really standards and falls lying flat together, and peony-style flowers which have 9-12 petals. The natural colour range was originally limited to white and shades of red-violet, blue and purple without markings. This was perhaps because these flowers were traditionally used in formal and ceremonial settings in which purity of colour and form were important. In recent years many hybrids have been produced with all sorts of markings and a wider range of exotic colours. In Japan and the USA also, induced tetraploids have been developed and we may expect some truly gargantuan flowers from them.

It has long been thought that these Japanese irises could be grown only in water or really boggy conditions, but this is not so. They need an acid soil, completely free from lime, and rich in organic matter. They are heavy feeders and should be mulched regularly with well-rotted manure and they must be given abundant moisture during the growing season. They are normally disease-free and the only attention required, other than watering and feeding, is the removal of dead foliage before the spring growth begins.

Planting is best done in the mid-autumn but it can be delayed until the early spring. Every three years the plants should be divided by the back-to-back fork method and replanted with the rhizomes at a depth of about 7-8 cm (3-4 ins). Japanese irises are late flowering and will not only provide a truly exotic display but will extend the iris season by several weeks.

Finally for our woodland setting there are a number of the mainly water-loving irises which will flourish with the Japanese. There are the Louisiana hybrids, the various forms of *I.chrysographes*, *I.forrestii* and *I.wilsonii* and other bog-lovers which will be dealt with in the next chapter.

CHAPTER 5

Irises for Water and Bog Gardens

It is not surprising that irises are so often associated with water gardens since the best known species is probably the water loving 'yellow flag' or *I.pseudacorus*. This graceful flower has long been a feature of the countryside, growing wild along river banks and in damp meadows throughout the temperate regions of Europe and Asia. Although, as we have seen, the *bearded* irises prefer warm and dry conditions, there are many *beardless* species which revel in wet situations and are ideal for the water garden.

Of these there are just a few which are entirely aquatic and will grow at their best only if under water to some extent. There are others which delight in thoroughly boggy conditions and yet more which will grow well enough in normal border conditions but even better in a moist environment. So there are irises which are ideal for all types of water gardens. With their graceful, sword-like and almost evergreen foliage they fit in beautifully with other water-side plants and the pure colours and exotic forms of the flowers will add delight to any water scene. Furthermore, they are all easy to grow. These are not the 'difficult' species, requiring special and expert attention through the year — they are easy going, good humoured and good mixers and, once established, require little attention and will increase in beauty from year to year.

With one or two exceptions they prefer soil which is more or less free of lime. In chalky areas, therefore, it may be necessary to acidify the topsoil, but only in extreme cases will they fail altogether. Again, with a few exceptions, they like an open, sunny position. We have seen that there are a few irises which will do well in the semi-shade, but most of the swamp and meadow dwellers like to be out in the open and have room to spread their roots. So we should avoid the overhanging trees and the root-infested banks of streams and try for a nice sunny spot.

Few of us are lucky enough to have a lake, or a river bank or a running stream in the garden, but much can be done by artificial means to create attractive water gardens. Formal and informal pools can be constructed in a number of ways and what was once a complex operation is simpler these days with the availability of fibreglass linings. In the shallow pockets which are usually formed at the edges of such pools our true aquatic irises will flourish. But a pool is not absolutely essential for them and suitable conditions can be created by forming an artificial 'swamp'. This can be done quite easily by digging a hole about 50 cm (20 ins) deep and a metre (3 ft 3 ins) or so square and lining it with heavy-grade polythene sheeting. If the soil is stony a layer of sand should be put down before the sheeting is laid. A further layer of sand should be spread over the sheeting and the whole thing two-thirds filled with lime-free compost and flooded to the brim with water. Kept topped up from time to time this will be ideal for the real water irises. Such a swamp should be easy to maintain and keep free of weed and if it should eventually spring a leak the whole thing can be renovated without much difficulty.

For the bulk of the moisture-loving irises the ideal situation is a slightly sloping bank along the water's edge, for they enjoy the damp atmosphere of such a position. Failing such a natural situation we must create a similar environment. We need to aim at producing a soil structure which is retentive of moisture but which, at the same time, allows the surplus water to drain away and not become stagnant. Few bog plants will survive stagnant conditions and certainly not irises. If the subsoil is very compacted then double digging is advisable to open up the ground and then the application of massive quantities of humus-forming materials well worked into the top 15 cm (6 ins) of the soil. Peat, leafmould and well-rotted farmyard manure would be suitable, supplemented by bone meal, hoof and horn or a good general fertiliser. Given such conditions and, of course, plenty of water, the plants will do magnificently and need little further attention.

Water Irises

The irises which will grow and flower when actually in water can be distinguished by the fact that the leaves have rows of tiny black cells running down the veins which show when a leaf is held to the light. Dykes called these 'watermarks' — a sure indication that the plants would tolerate flood conditions.

Of this group there is only one, *I.laevigata*, which simply must be grown in water if it is to flourish. This most beautiful of irises was described by Dykes as 'the finest blue iris that we possess'. It is native to Eastern Asia, China, Korea and Japan, where it is abundant and has been grown and loved for centuries under the name Kakitsubata. It is the blue 'Japanese iris' which is so well known in Japanese prints, on screens and in other works of art. It was discovered in Siberia in 1770 by Pallas. It is closely related to *I.ensata* with which it is often to be found in the wild and with which it is often confused. The two species differ in several ways. *I.ensata* has a pronounced mid-rib on the leaf, whereas the leaf of *I.laevigata* is quite smooth and is also rather wider. The flowers of *I.ensata* are red-purple but those of *I.laevigata* are a true deep blue while another important difference is that *I.laevigata* flowers two or three weeks earlier than *I.ensata*.

The flowers are borne at a height of 35 cm (14 ins) on slender stems inclined to zigzag and with three or four flowers which emerge successively from large green spathes. It flowers in early summer, at roughly the same time as the tall bearded, and if the seed pods are removed will often flower again in the autumn. For its roots it needs about 25-30 cm (10-12 ins) of soil (or mud) under water and it can be grown in large pots or tubs with their tops 10 cm (4 ins) under water. Frequent division is not necessary but congestion may result in a lessening in the number of flower spikes. Planting and division can be done at any time between spring and autumn, but never in the winter months. The leaves will die down in the winter but will not disappear entirely. The essentials for success are water and sunshine and the rewards are large and ornamental flowers of the richest colour. Apart from the type there are a number of good varieties of *I.laevigata*: var. *alba* is a less than vigorous white, faintly mottled with blue; var. *albopurpurea* has mainly white flowers mottled with purple and is a vigorous grower with large handsome flowers; var. *montrosa* is something of a curiosity with flowers half white, mottled blue and half blue; var. *variegata* has foliage strongly marked with white or pale yellow stripes and pale purple/blue flowers. All are well worth growing.

We come now to the yellow water-flag, *I.pseudacorus*, which grows wild throughout Europe and North Asia and is at its best in really watery situations. Being a vigorous grower it is best suited to large areas of meadow or the river bank and should be used with great care in small gardens. In formal ponds it can be grown in sunken containers with dramatic effect but is most suitable for large-scale water gardens. This is the only true water iris with yellow flowers, which are usually veined in brown with a brown blotch on the falls. They are carried on tall stems, 100 cms (3 ft 3 ins) or more, and appear in mid-summer. The foliage is robust, bright green and rather coarse. The large seed pods are of a glossy, deep green and are much in demand for floral decoration. The plant needs virtually no attention apart from the removal of dead leaves and an occasional mulch with farmyard manure. The seed pods should be removed before they burst open, otherwise you will have a garden full of yellow flags.

There is a white form var. *alba*, which is less vigorous but is difficult to obtain. It is well worth a search. The variety *bastardii* is a very attractive form which has pale, lemon-yellow flowers which are more elegantly shaped than the type and do not have the brown blotch. The variety *acoriformis* has yellow flowers and a deeper yellow blotch. The variety *variegata* is exceptionally attractive as a tall foliage plant with lovely gold and green-striped leaves, but the variegations seem to disappear in the late summer. Tetraploid forms of *I.pseudacorus* have now been developed and who knows what gigantic varieties of this already vigorous species may arise?

Another group of water irises comes from the USA. *I.versicolor* is the American equivalent of *I.pseudacorus* to which it is similar in size, vigour and habit, but the flowers are blue-purple in light-to-dark shades and with purple veining. There is a most attractive form, *kermesina*, which has wine-red flowers. A more slender form, *I.virginica*, is usually taller and less well-branched and has blue-purple flowers at 60-90 cm (2-3 ft). Yet another form, *I.shrevei*, is less tall, 45-60 cm (18-24 ins), and has flowers of mixed colours from purple through to white. These are the commonest native irises of the north-eastern USA and they really deserve to be more widely grown in other parts of the world. Their hardiness, generous branching, ease of growing and colourful and graceful flowers make them splendid water garden plants.

One more true water-lover is the newcomer 'Gerald Darby'. This is most unusual as its blue-purple flowers of the Siberian type are carried on long, twisted, dark red-purple stems. It was originally thought to have been a cross between *I.orientalis* and two Louisiana hybrids but is more likely to have been a chance seedling and a form of *I.versicolor*. It is well worth a place in any water garden but needs plenty of room as it is very vigorous.

It should be emphasised that, with the exception of *laevigata*, all these irises will also grow quite well in the bog garden or herbaceous border, though with perhaps less vigour. They all have fairly large rhizomes and are best propagated by division. They can be split up into clumps, or separate rhizomes can be planted provided there are two or three good shoots. For growing in water, planting is best done in the late spring and for the bog garden or border, in the autumn. As we leave the true water irises we should refer again to the Japanese irises (*I.ensata*) which were described in Chapter 4 as woodland plants. They are often associated with water gardens and look especially attractive in a watery setting. They can be very effective against a background of water when grown in pots. A large tray is required, at least 10 cm (4 ins) deep half filled in the spring with rainwater (not tap water). The irises should be planted either as single fans or small clumps in 25-cm (10 in) pots which stand in the water. The pots should be two-thirds filled with a very much enriched compost composed of lime-free John Innes compost, peat and well-rotted farmyard manure in equal parts. In the autumn

Figure 5.1
Iris versicolor

Figure 5.2
Iris ensata

and the spring a mulch of the same mixture 3-5 cm (1½-2 ins) deep should be applied and when the pots are full the plants can be repotted or even divided. Division and planting is best done in the spring. This treatment is suitable for both indoors and outside in the garden.

Irises for the Bog and Border

We come now to the rich, moist border for which there is a wide range of irises in addition to those already mentioned. A most attractive group are the Louisiana irises. These are native to the bayou country of southern Louisiana around New Orleans. Here in the springtime the salt marshes are remarkable for drifts of these flowers in almost all the colours of the rainbow. Botanically they are of the series Hexagonae, so named from their six-ribbed ovaries and capsules, and there are now five recognised species:

Figure 5.3
Iris sibirica 'Snow Crest'

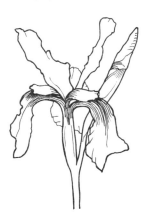

Louisiana Iris

I.brevicaulis (originally known as *I.foliosa*) is the smallest species in the group with bright blue flowers usually hidden in the foliage at a height of about 15-30 cm (6-12 ins). The flowers, with horizontal falls and upright standards are carried on the zigzag stems which are characteristic of the whole group and as many as six may open at one time. They are specially suitable as edging plants. *I.fulva* has flowers of a coppery red colour with drooping falls and standards on almost straight stems 45-60 cm (18-24 ins) tall. By crossing *I.fulva* with *I.brevicaulis* (which he knew as *lamancei*) Dykes produced a fine hybrid with blue purple flowers and of vigorous growth. This proved to be fertile and was given specific status as *I.fulvala*. It is now regarded as a hybrid but is a very good garden plant.
I.giganticaerulea is a magnificent tall species with violet-purple or white flowers with broad flaring falls and upright standards, carried at different levels on stems up to 80 cm (2 ft 8 ins) tall. *I.hexagona* itself is less widely grown and has rather undistinguished greenish-white and purple flowers on 90-cm (3 ft) stems. *I.nelsonii* is a giant fulva type with red-purple or yellow flowers on 60-90 cm (2-3 ft) stems. Magnificent specimens were found in the 1930s in the Vermilion Bay area near to Abbeville and they became famous as the 'Abbeville Reds'.

From these species there have been developed in the USA a series of spectacular hybrids which vary in height from 50 to 100 cm (20 ins - 3 ft 3 ins), with flowers as wide as 20 cm (8 ins). They are most elegant in form; the range of colours and patterns is very wide and the variety of flower form is equally diverse. They have a long flowering period and are eminently worth growing.

For the best growth and development they must have food and moisture in the spring and autumn; they do best where they have the sun for at least half the day, but the rhizomes need to be protected from the direct rays of the sun in hot weather. They should be planted in the late autumn with the rhizomes not deeper than 5 cm (2 ins) and heavily mulched. Propagation of these Louisiana irises is very easy. The very long rhizomes can be split down the centre and then cut into short pieces 3-5 cm (1½-2 ins) long. Planted in peat and sand they will quickly root and send out shoots and should flower in two years. The hybrids are vigorous growers and should be planted out with a space of at least 50 cm (20 ins) otherwise they will soon grow into each other.

Next for our moist border there is a range of species which require lime-free conditions. Those of the Chrysographes series offer a wide variety of most delightful flowers of delicate colour and form:

I.bulleyana, blue-purple flowers with a touch of yellow on the falls — 45 cm (18 ins). Named as a species by Dykes but may well be a natural hybrid.

I.chrysographes, one of the loveliest of all irises. It has narrow petalled flowers at 35 cm (14 ins) of deep velvety red-violet and the falls have golden lines and dots. The colour can range from near black to true red-violet. The form *rubella* is rather shorter and has bright red-violet flowers.

Figure 5.4
Iris chrysographes

I.delavayi, is the tallest of the series — 90-130 cm (3 ft- 4 ft 4 ins) — with dark-purple flowers with white or yellow signals.

I.clarkei is unusual in having solid rather than hollow stems which are well branched. The flowers are blue-purple with nearly horizontal standards. 60 cm (2 ft).

I.dykesii is a larger version of *I.chrysographes* with dark violet flowers with a yellow signal. It was named for Dykes by Stapf but its origin is unknown.

I.forrestii has yellow flowers with purple-brown lines and dots — 30-45 cm (12-18 ins).

I.wilsonii has pale yellow flowers with brown veining. 60 cm.

All these charming irises are native to Eastern Asia and China.

Other irises requiring lime-free moist conditions are:

I.setosa. This very attractive flower is virtually three-petalled, as the standards are almost non-existent, and is like a miniature blue-purple form of *I.pseudacorus*. About 25-40 cm (10-16 ins) high. Hybrids of *I.setosa* and *I.laevigata* are in existence and are well worth searching for as they look like dwarf Japanese irises and are easy growing and vigorous.

I.prismatica, another unusual species which has very elegantly branched solid stems and prettily marked flowers of purple and white, pale violet or white. 45-60 cm (18-24 ins).

There are a number of hybrids between the Californian group and the Chrysographes group (Cal/Sib. hybrids) which will do well in moist, lime-free conditions. The best known of these is the wine-red 'Margot Holmes', which won the first-ever Dykes Medal in 1927. Finally for this situation *I.missouriensis* and *I.lactea*, which have already been described, will do well in areas of the border which are not too wet.

The cultivation of all these irises is very easy — they simply need to be kept moist and mulched with peat in the spring. They prefer not to be disturbed, but if the clumps become too big they can be divided two months after flowering and smaller clumps replanted 10 cm (4 ins) deep and 25 cm (10 ins) apart.

There are, in addition, for the moist border irises which will not object to lime in the soil:

I.sibirica, one of the oldest known species. Native to central Europe and Russia it has tall graceful foliage and branched stems 60-90 cm (2-3 ft) high. The flowers are blue-violet heavily marked with white streaks.

I.sanguinea, from eastern Asia, is similar but has unbranched stems and the white markings on the flowers are less pronounced. In both species the falls are drooping, but from these have been developed a vast range of hybrids and the modern tendency has been to produce near-horizontal flaring falls and some ruffling. Hybrids exist in many colours, white and shades of blue-violet and purple and near blue, and efforts continue to produce a true yellow. The many named cultivars of this group make splendid garden plants.

In the USA and in Germany, tetraploid Siberian irises have been raised which are quite dramatic. They have thicker, more upright leaves, much longer stems and huge flowers — up to 15 cm diameter — of heavier substance and with broad flaring falls.

One or two of the irises already recommended for the mixed border can also be used effectively in the damp situation to add variety and extend the flowering period. The graceful *I.longipetala* enjoys extra moisture, so long as the drainage is good. Some of the Spurias, also, will flourish and are useful as they flower later than most others. *Orientalis, halophila, monnieri* and *spuria* itself will give a colour range of white/yellow, yellow and pale blue.

Finally for the moist border there is an unusual iris well worth looking out for. It is a natural hybrid which was discovered in a nursery in Yorkshire and is believed to be a cross between *I.chryso-graphes* and *I.foetidissima*. It was named 'Holden Clough' to commemorate the nursery where it was found. The flower is yellow, closely veined purple, giving a general brown effect and there is a yellow spot on the falls. It flowers at about 75 cm (2 ft 6 ins), is an excellent grower and very floriferous. It is quite unlike any other iris and most desirable.

Figure 5.5 (Plan 7) shows a suggested layout of beardless irises in a border with wet clay soil.

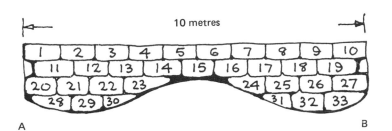

Figure 5.5
A Border of
Beardless Irises in
Wet Clay Soil
(Plan 7)
Ground sloping
down from A to B

1 *I.milesii* reddish-purple
2 *I.sib.* 'Tycoon' violet
3 *I.sib.* 'Orville Fay' blue
4 *I.sib.* 'Limeheart' white
5 *Japanese* 'Star at Midnight' purple double
6 *Japanese* 'Numazu' white single
7 *I.spur.* 'Driftwood' brown
8 *I.spur.* 'Wadi Zem Zem' cream white
9 *I.spur.* 'Port of Call' violet blue
10 *I.pseudacorus variegata*
11 *I.sib.* 'Cambridge' blue
12 *I.sib.* 'Nottingham Lace' wine/white
13 *I.sib.* 'White Swirl' white
14 *I.sib.* 'Eric the Red' wine
15 *I.foetidissima variegata*
16 *I.lae.* 'Gerald Darby' deep blue
17 *I.sib/setosa* 'Stille Wasser' blue
18 *I.spur.* 'Morning Tide' blueish-white
19 *I.spur.* 'Elixir' gold
20 *I.unguicularis*
21 *I.versicolor*
22 'Holden Clough' brown
23 *I.longipetala*
24 *I.setosa*
25 *I.chrysographes* black
26 *I.sib.* 'Anniversary' white
27 *I.ensata variegata*
28 *I.cal/sib.* 'Margot Holmes' wine
29 *I.cal.* 'No Name' yellow
30 *I.lactea*
31 *I.kerneriana*
32 *I.fulva*
33 *I.ruthenica*

CHAPTER 6

Irises for the Rock Garden, Scree and Hot, Dry Border

In this chapter we deal with a wide variety of irises which will be at their best in the rock garden, on scree slopes and in hot, dry borders, and many of which will also do well in other situations with similar growing conditions. They are mainly the smaller species which look especially lovely in rocky surroundings and enjoy the good drainage of such environments.

Bearded Irises First and foremost there are the smaller bearded irises, the miniature dwarf bearded (MDB) and the standard dwarf bearded (SDB), which will provide fine splashes of colour in the spring. They are specially suitable for the rockery as they delight in the hot pockets of soil between the stones and will spread happily to form drifts and cascades of great beauty. They require the same treatment in cultivation as the tall bearded but they do not need such frequent division. They can normally be left in the same position for some four or five years without harm.

The MDBs are the first of the bearded irises to flower — in April in the United Kingdom — and they have one or two flowers on stems up to 20 cm (8 ins) with the flowers held just above the leaves. They may be divided and moved between mid-summer and spring. In addition to the many very delightful cultivars which are readily available there are a number of interesting species and we list the following which are reliable and a joy to grow on the rockery:

I.alexeenkoi has a single blue flower with a yellow beard — about
    20 cm (8 ins).
I.chamaeiris is one of the best known species, often confused with
    I.pumila from which it differs in having a longer stem (up to
    20 cm) and a short perianth tube. There are many colour forms,
    purple, violet, yellow and white.
I.furcata has a branched stem with purple flowers and can be as tall
    as 45 cm (18 ins).
I.mellita has one to three brown-purple flowers with hardly any
    stem. An unusual species which likes a sheltered spot and may
    need protection in a hard winter.
I.pumila has a very short stem and a long perianth tube and a wide

colour range, purple, violet, blue, yellow and white. Used in
hybridising to produce the modern dwarf iris cultivars.

I.reichenbachii has one or two beautifully marked yellow or
brownish-purple flowers. 15-25 cm (6-10 ins).

I.timofejewii has one purple/violet flower with a white beard.
15 cm.

The SDBs are more robust than the MDBs and flower about two
weeks later. They often have branched stems about 20-40 cm
(8-16 ins) and are very floriferous. There are now very many fine
named varieties in a wonderful range of colour and pattern combinations. They cannot be too highly recommended for the rock
garden or the edge of the sunny border and no garden should be
without them. Hardy, easy to grow, disease free and so beautiful —
what more can be asked of a flowering plant? For those who enjoy
growing the species, those we list are very rewarding and are among
the oldest known irises:

I.aphylla has three to five purple flowers on well branched stems —
15-45 cm (6-18 ins) — will sometimes flower again in the autumn.

I.lutescens has two or three pale yellow flowers, beautifully scented,
on a 25-cm (10 in)-stem. Vigorous and floriferous it is long
lasting and, seen in drifts, an absolute joy to behold.

I.olbiensis has two or three whitish-green flowers on a 20-cm stem,
often well branched.

These three give a complete range of the basic colours in this group.
A more recently identified species well worth looking for is

I.schactii, which has unusual greenish-yellow flowers, rather like
a miniature *I.imbricata* and blooms rather earlier than the others.

For the open areas in the rock garden and for the scree and
border slightly larger irises can be grown effectively. These are the
intermediates and miniature tall bearded groups. The intermediates
have 40-70 cm (16 ins-2 ft 4 ins) stems, good branching and flower
in profusion a little later than the SDBs. There are many fine
modern cultivars giving a full range of colours and patterns. There
are, also, of course, the famous old varieties which have long been
thought of as species but are now reduced to the status of varieties,
such as the various forms of *germanica*, *albicans* and so on. We
suggest that of this group no one should fail to grow:

'Florentina', the lovely 'orris root' plant which has delicately scented
flowers of bluish-white on well-branched stems 38-45 cm

(15-18 ins) tall. Apart from its great historical interest this is also a first-class garden plant.

'Kochii'. This is a specially useful plant. Although the flowers are rather floppy in form they are of unusual colour, a rich deep violet-purple, with at least four flowers to a stem, 45 cm (18 ins) tall. 'Kochii' will often rebloom in the autumn and even in the middle of winter. It is an extremely vigorous grower and almost evergreen.

The miniature tall bearded irises are strongly recommended for the rock garden, not only because they contrast so charmingly with the rugged stony background, but also because they flower later than the intermediates and thus extend the season. They were originally known as 'table irises' from their obvious suitability for table decoration. They have slender, very well branched stems, with small, beautifully formed flowers at a height of not more than 70 cm (2 ft 4 ins). The foliage is slight and in every way they are miniature with a dainty and delicate character all their own. They have long been neglected but a number of fine varieties are now available and they very much deserve a place in any iris collection. They derived originally from a small group of species native to the Balkans of which the two oldest are:

I.cengialti, which carries up to six scented blue-violet flowers at about 30-40 cm (12-16 ins).

I.variegata, which normally has a mass of flowers on well-branched stems. They have bright-yellow standards and very heavily veined falls giving an appearance of red-brown. This iris played a major part in the development of the modern TB but is most attractive in itself and well worth growing.

There are a number of other irises suitable for the sunny rockery or scree. The group known as Psammiris are found in the wild in sandy, gritty situations on the mountains from Central Europe, through Transcaucasian Russia to Mongolia and Manchuria. They are distinguished by having slightly stoloniferous rhizomes and small white arils on the seeds, and by the strange way in which the withering flowers twist into spirals. They are low growing, not above 20 cm (8 ins), and the short-lived flowers are bright yellow attractively veined in brown-purple. There is confusion about the naming of the recognised species but the ones to look out for are popularly known as *I.arenaria*, *I.flavissima* and *I.mandschurica*.

Another group for the sandy scree are the Pseudoregelias, which will be dealt with more fully in the next chapter. They are really alpine species and come from the Himalayas, Mongolia and Siberia.

They are short in growth, not above 15 cm (6 ins), and have one or two unusually formed mauve to purple flowers beautifully mottled with darker purple spots. The species to go for in this group are *I.kamaonensis*, *I.sikkimmensis* and *I.tigridia*, the last of which can have either blue-purple or yellow flowers.

Among the beardless irises which delight in a hot, sandy scree are three very rare but lovely species from Eastern Asia which are worthy of specialist attention. They are of the Tenuifoliae sub-section and have thin, wiry rhizomes and short, thin stems with pale, blue-purple flowers. They are *I.loczyi*, *I.tenuifolia* and *I.ventricosa*.

Beardless Irises for the Rockery and Scree

All these sand-loving irises need little attention once they are established but they like to have some moisture during the growing season and to remain dry thereafter. If, therefore, they are in positions where water may drip on them in the winter they should be covered with open-sided cloches.

A good subject for the front of the rock garden is the dwarf form of *I.unguicularis* known as *I.cretensis*. The tiny flower of soft lilac with gold markings appears low in the long, very thin leaves which spring from short-jointed rhizomes. This is a sun-lover and should be planted in the open and is best left undisturbed. It will not mind a fairly heavy loam soil provided it is not water-logged. It will flower delightfully in early spring and should be planted close to a path where it can be seen and enjoyed.

Figure 6.1
Iris reticulata,
Iris histrioides
and *Iris histrio*

The bulbous irises are, on the whole, excellent for use in the rock garden and sunny border and will enjoy the warm soil among the stones and should naturalise happily. They need to be labelled very

65

carefully as they die down completely in the early summer and reappear only in the late winter when they begin to flower. It is so easy to forget just where they are. The smaller bulbous irises of the Reticulata section are the earliest to flower and are best planted in the autumn, 5 cm (2 ins) deep and 5 cm apart in groups. They should be given a good dressing of dried blood in the spring — say a handful for each group. There are a number of splendid named varieties easily obtainable in wide variations of light and deep blue, red-purple, purple and violet. The species are wonderfully varied and the following should be grown:

I.bakerana, violet and white bitone with white and occasionally orange ridges on the falls.

I.danfordiae, a yellow self of robust growth. (The bulbs should be planted more deeply than the others, say 15 cm (6 ins), and heavily fed at the outset since, after flowering, they tend to split up into small bulblets which may take up to three years to reach flowering size. They should be carefully marked and left undisturbed and (with luck and a little prayer!) should produce a nice drift in due time).

I.histrioides, of which the original form is seldom grown, but the variety 'Major' is one of the best and most reliable of the group. The flowers are large and of a wonderful ultramarine colour. One of the absolute 'musts'.

I.reticulata, the type species, blue-violet and very good.

I.winogradowii, pale yellow and late flowering.

The Reticulatas all have flowers about 5 cm (2 ins) tall which appear in the early spring before the leaves get going. They like a neutral soil and good drainage. They are susceptible to their own special disease, 'Ink Spot', a fungus which develops in moist conditions and can be fatal. At the first sign of spots on the leaves they should be soaked in a strong fungicide. Badly infected plants should be burnt.

The larger bulbous irises of the *Xiphium* sub-genus are best known as florists' flowers but the species from which the Dutch iris derived can be attractively used for the sun-baked border or sunny shelves in the rock garden.

I.xiphium itself is variable in colour and has yellow or orange patches on the falls.

I.tingitana is an early blooming species with large light-blue flowers and yellow signals.

I.fontanesii is a later blooming and more slender version of *I.tingitana*.

The bulbs should be planted in the late autumn, 10 cm (4 ins) deep and 5-10 cm (2-4 ins) apart.

I.tuberosa

An unusual plant which likes a sunny border or a sheltered corner on the rockery is the so called 'Widow Iris' or 'Snake's Head Iris' which we recognise as a separate sub-genus *Hermodactylus*. It differs from other irises in having a fleshy, tuberous rootstock. It resembles the *reticulata* in flower and is most attractive with yellowish-green standards and dark purplish-black falls. It likes a rich soil and, once established, should be left undisturbed.

The Juno irises are dealt with fully in Chapter 7 since most of them are best suited to the bulb frame, but there are six of the more robust species of this section which will flourish in and greatly adorn the dry, sunny border. These unusual and little-known plants have foliage rather like that of sweet corn and delicate flowers which often emerge from the axils of the leaves. They have bulbs similar to those of Dutch irises but with long, fleshy roots which it is important not to break when transplanting. They like a very rich, dry, sandy loam with plenty of organic manure and peat incorporated. They are tolerant of slightly damp positions but do not like to have their 'necks' frozen when wet. In frosty weather, therefore, they should be protected with cloches. Given this attention the following should grow well out of doors and give great pleasure:

I.aucheri is early flowering, 30 cm (12 ins) high with flowers from white to clear blue.

I.bucharica is the commonest form, 40 cm (16 ins) high with cream flowers and patches of yellow on the falls.

I.cycloglossa has handsome flowers with flaring falls of a true blue colour, 60-90 cm (2-3 ft) or more.

I.graeberana has pale blue flowers, 35-40 cm (14-16 ins).

I.magnifica, a truly wonderful iris with strong, deep green foliage and 6 or 7 finely shaped flowers of white or pale violet in the axils of the upper leaves. 37-60 cm (15-24 ins). Another must for any garden.

I.orchioides, with its pale and deep-yellow flowers. 30 cm (12 ins).

Two other irises which are suitable for the rockery and are a little out of the ordinary are the crested species *I.tectorum*, which has already been described, and *I.japonica* var. *confusa*. The former requires plenty of feed and regular moving; the latter likes a rich humus and a sheltered frost-free position.

We move now from the sun-baked parts of the rock garden or border to the semi-shaded areas. For these the smaller species of the Spuria group have much to recommend them. They not only

The Semi-shaded Rockery

have a distinctive character in foliage and flowers but they need little attention and do not require to be disturbed for years. They like a good, rich, loamy soil, preferably without lime, and a fair amount of moisture in the growing season. They flower in mid to late summer and can be planted in either the spring or autumn. Most important is:

I.graminea, of which the flowers are basically white, very heavily veined with purple, giving a generally reddish-purple effect. The flowers are carried low in the fountain of slender leaves and are particularly useful as cut flowers. They have the sweet scent of plums or apricots and in olden times the plant was known as 'the plum-scented, narrow-leaved, iris'.

Other similar species in the series, giving a range of colours are:

I.brandzai, blue-purple. Scented.
I.kerneriana, straw-yellow flowers. Late flowering.
I.ludwigii, violet-blue and, unusually, with a slight beard.
I.sintenisii, cream background colour heavily veined in purple. Scented.
I.uromovii, deep blue-purple. Scented.

The flowers of all these are of characteristic Spuria form, very prettily marked, and carried at about 20-25 cm (8-10 ins). The foliage is flat and very narrow, giving a grass-like appearance and it dies down completely in the winter.

I.graminea is partial to the shade and with it can be grown the smaller Californian species which also do not like lime. We have already recommended them for the mixed border and for the rockery we suggest:

I.bracteata, pale yellow;
I.chrysophylla, cream, veined violet;
I.hartwegii, cream, purple and yellow;
I.purdyi, cream, veined purple;
I.tenuissima, cream or yellow, veined brown.

These are all comparatively low growing, 15-25 cm (6-10 ins), and will combine well with the Spuria species and, like them, prefer to be left undisturbed.

A few other lime-free irises which should find a place in the rock garden are these rather individual species:

I.verna, the tiny semi-bearded iris from the USA which likes a shady spot and has miniature pale-lilac flowers with an orange patch on the falls.

I.ruthenica. This unique species forms grass-like hummocks in the summer and has delicate pale-violet flowers, nicely scented, on thin stems about 20 cm (8 ins) long. It is shy to bloom and when division is necessary, this must be done in the summer when the plant is in full growth.

I.setosa. The miniature forms of this so-called three-petalled iris make good rock garden plants and the rich, near-blue and white flowers are very attractive.

I.minuto aurea. We mention this species almost as a challenge. The smallest of all the beardless irises, this native of Japan is very difficult to flower in temperate areas. It has perfectly formed miniature flowers, only 5-10 cm (2-4 ins) high, yellow with brown markings and should do well in a sheltered spot on the rockery with some overhead protection against too much moisture.

Finally, the shady, leafy scree between the rocks is ideal for a group of shade and damp-loving crested irises:

I.cristata and the smaller form *I.lacustris*, native of the USA, have delicate blue and white flowers on very short stems and grow from thin, wiry rhizomes.

I.tenuis, a larger version of *I.cristata* with purple-veined white flowers about 20 cm (8 ins) high.

I.gracilipes, from Japan, has tiny, truly exquisite lilac flowers on thin branching stems. 15-20 cm (6-8 ins).

These all flower in the early spring and should be left undisturbed until the rhizomes become really matted. Then division must be done immediately after flowering.

Irises for Stone Paths

'Flag' irises and flagstone paths have long been associated alike in cottage gardens and in more formal layouts. The paths themselves can be enriched by growing in the wide joints some of the delightful miniature irises. For dry spots there are the various colour forms of *I.pumila*; its near relative *I.attica*, which has greenish-yellow flowers with a brown signal patch and *I.mellita*, with most delicate brown-purple flowers. For the shady corner there is the quite dazzling *I.verna* and in the peaty nook, *I.cristata* can be tried. For very early flowering the small bulbous *I.reticulata* and *I.histrioides* are very suitable.

Sink Gardens

Well-drained sinks are suitable for the growing of irises, and although stone sinks are the best looking, any type can in fact be used and even cement sinks will do (except for the lime-haters). A good soil mixture is John Innes No. 3 compost, or Levington compost and 'pea' grit in equal quantities by bulk with the addition of 'Seagold' or 'Phostrogen' of the appropriate strength, all well mixed together.

For the normal shallow sink suitable subjects are the small bulbous irises of the *reticulata* group; the crested *I.cristata*, *I.lacustris* and *I.gracilipes*; *I.verna* and the dwarf form of *I.setosa*; the less vigorous hybrids of *I.innominata* and the dwarf *spurias*, *I.sintenisii* and *I.uromovii*. *I.ruthenica* can also be tried. For the deeper sink the smaller bearded irises, MDBs and SDBs can be used as well. If a really deep horse-trough is available the scope is greatly increased. In the bearded range the miniature tall bearded irises would be especially good, together with the smaller IBs, the regeliocyclus and the smaller arilbreds. Some of the slightly taller *spurias* such as *I.graminea* and *I.kerneriana* will extend the flowering season. We can also include some of the Californian tribe such as *I.fernaldii*, *I.hartwegii* and *I.tenuissima* though these may need a little protection from frost. Finally, and ideally for the deep sink, we must put in a word for our great favourite *I.lactea*).

CHAPTER 7

Irises for the Bulb Frame and the Alpine House

We examine first of all some ways in which bulb frames suitable for irises can be made and we illustrate the basic design in Figure 7.1. The object of the frame is to provide a sheltered environment with good ventilation and with soil of which the top layer can be kept completely dry when required and which can be watered from below at the appropriate time. Such frames are best sited in a sheltered but not shaded position, preferably against a south-facing wall.

The first operation is to dig a hole of the appropriate size, about 50 cm (20 ins) deep, and fill it in with rubble. A stone wall should then be built around the hole to a height of 60-75 cm (2 ft-2 ft 6 ins) and filled in with, first, a layer of turfs, very well-rotted cow manure and old compost, and then the soil which was dug out, mixed with 'pea' grit for drainage, old mushroom compost and some bone meal. A perforated water pipe should be laid in the soil, about 25 cm (10 ins) below the surface, with a controlling valve outside, protected from the frost. A framework should then be erected, of wood or metal, supporting a sloping cover of clear, corrugated plastic, with an overlap of 50 cm at the sides and back and 25 cm at the front. Care must be taken in the design and siting to ensure that the wind will not drive the rain onto the plants.

As an alternative to the home-made framework suggested, a standard commercial metal garden frame with sliding glass panels can be used, seated on the stone wall. If you can find a large horse trough, this could well be used instead of the stone wall surround, but care must be taken to form really adequate drainage holes.

Another form of construction is to sink the stone wall half into the ground with, say, 30 cm (12 ins) below the ground and 30 cm above. Open joints should be left in the bottom course of stones below the ground to allow water to get in and out. In this case watering from below will occur naturally and though we recommend the provision of a water supply pipe as before, it may be needed only in very dry spring seasons.

With a bulb frame such as we have described there is a capability of growing a greatly extended range of irises, including the more 'difficult' species in the small bulbous section, the Junos, the Regelias and even the exotic and most rewarding Oncocyclus.

Figure 7.1
Iris Bulb Frame

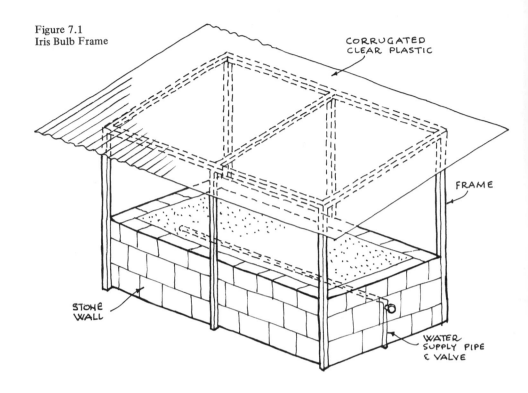

CORRUGATED
CLEAR PLASTIC

FRAME

STONE
WALL

WATER
SUPPLY PIPE
& VALVE

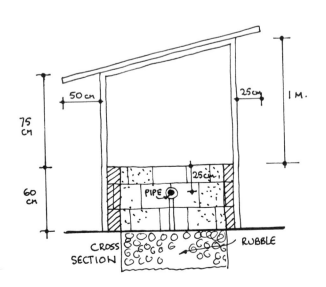

50 cm

25 cm

1 M.

75
CM

60
CM

25 cm

PIPE

CROSS
SECTION

RUBBLE

Irises for the Bulb Frame and the Alpine House

We have already seen that a number of the small bulbous irises of the Reticulata section will do well in a woodland setting and in the dry border and rock garden, but they will do even better in the frame where they will be protected from the most severe frost and from being eaten by birds and mice. In this situation they can be expected to form quite large clumps in next to no time. The various named varieties of *I.reticulata* itself may be grown; the lovely blue *histrioides* and its forms, which flower early before the leaves are fully developed and also *I.danfordiae*, which needs to be heavily fed with dried blood to make the bulbs up to flowering size in following years. In addition there are the following less easy species which are of surpassing beauty:

I.bakerana, a miniature bitone with violet-blue standards and deep blue and white, veined falls. Fragrant and early flowering. Parent of several fine hybrids such as 'Clairette' and 'Pauline'.

I.histrio, blue and greenish-white, often dramatically marked in deep blue-violet. Very early flowering.

I.kolpakowskiana, a very striking flower, named in 1877 for a governor of Turkestan. Light-purple standards and veined falls of purple, white and yellow, with distinctive, crocus-like foliage.

I.pamphylica, more recently discovered in Turkey. A bicolour with pale-violet and brown standards and green/brown falls. Late flowering.

I.vartani, the earliest of the section to flower. Slaty-blue veined standards and veined lilac falls with a yellow crest. The white form,

I.vartani alba is more easily obtainable. In addition to their delicate beauty, both forms of *I.vartani* have a delightful almond scent.

I.winogradowii, a short-stemmed yellow self which flowers very late. A rare and delicate species which, like *reticulata*, should also do well in the dry border, but its cost will probably preclude reckless planting. The bulbs do not break up like those of *I.danfordiae*.

As with many of the species described in this chapter, these are not easy to obtain commercially, as nurserymen naturally tend to concentrate on those which are easiest to grow. They are, however, real treasures, very well worth seeking out and a joy to bring into flower.

Of the larger bulbous irises of the sub-genus Xiphium, the Spanish, Dutch and English irises will grow well outside as we have already described, but there are some special species in this group which are treasures also, and will do best in the frame:

Figure 7.2
Dutch Iris

I.boissieri, the only bearded iris in this group. Blue-purple and yellow with a distinctive yellow beard. 30 cm (12 ins).

I.filifolia, red-purple with a yellow signal patch. 37 cm (15 ins).

I.fontanesii, a dark-blue, rather slender form of tingitana. Late flowering. 60 cm (2 ft).

I.juncea, yellow scented flowers and distinctive rushlike leaves. 30 cm.

I.serotina, violet flowers with only vestigeal standards. Late flowering. 30-35 cm (12-14 ins).

I.tingitana, a 'difficult' species. A very lovely pale blue with veining. Flowers very early and requires very heavy feeding and protection from late frosts. A parent of the famous Dutch iris 'Wedgewood'.

The Junos

Figure 7.3
A Fine Juno Iris –
I.bucharica

The last of the bulbous irises to be mentioned are the Junos. We have already described the members of this section which will grow out of doors. There are many more which will beautify the bulb frame in the spring and give the greatest joy. Though not the most exotic of flowers they have a delicate and exquisite character of their own and the foliage, too, is distinctive and attractive. The leaves emerge from the central stems rather like leeks or sweet corn, and the dainty flowers come up on short stems from the leaf axils. The plants range in height from 10 to 90 cm (4 ins to 3 ft). The smaller Junos will grow well in the bulb frame but are at their best in the alpine house.

In the cultivation of the Junos it is specially important to simulate the conditions in which the species grow in the wild. Planting should be done in the autumn and the soil should be heavily fed with an organic fertiliser. The bulbs should be put in at a depth of 10 cm (4 ins) to make sure that they do not get frozen. Great care must be taken not to break off the long-food-storing roots otherwise the plants will be very much weakened. When in growth, overhead watering must be avoided since these plants are likely to rot if they get wet around the neck, and even more they dislike being frozen at soil level. After flowering they should be given a good mulch of old mushroom compost with added superphosphate of lime. From then onwards to the next growing season the frame should be kept dry to allow the bulb to ripen in the maximum warmth of the sun. Watering should be from below and the plants should be fed annually with a mixture of bone meal, or hoof and horn, and sulphate of potash.

For the complete list of the Juno species we must refer you to the classification in Appendix VI but will mention here those which are easiest to grow and available commercially. Of these we

74

have already described three very lovely species *I.bucharica*, *I.graebe-rana* and *I.magnifica* which are hardier than most and will flourish in the open as well as in the frame. Other real beauties which are obtainable are:

I.aucheri, known also as *I.sindjarensis*. Pale blue, white or smoky-grey. 30 cm (12 ins).
I.caucasica, pale yellow with a deeper yellow crest. 15 cm (6 ins).
I.orchioides, pale and deep yellow with an orange crest. 30 cm.
I.persica occurs in many colours, the more usual form being pale greenish-blue with a purple blotch at the end of the falls. The variety *sieheana* is most often found and is a pale grey-blue with maroon falls. Very short, about 5 cm (2 ins). *I.persica* is a truly delightful miniature Juno and has the great distinction of having been the first plant illustrated and described in Curtis's *Botanical Magazine* of 1787. It is admittedly difficult to retain long in cultivation but well worth the effort.
I.willmottiana. The species is lavender, flushed with blue — 15 cm (6 ins) — but a better-known form is white with an orange blotch and this is sometimes winter hardy in the open.

Rather more vigorous and equally rewarding are two interesting hybrids which are quite widely grown:

'Sindpers', (*I.aucheri* or *sindjarensis* x *I.persica*) (Van Tubergen 1889). Greenish-blue with an orange crest. Free flowering.
'Warlsind', (*I.warleyensis* x *I.aucheri*) (Van Tubergen 1936). Deep blue and yellow bicolour. 25 cm (10 ins). Sometimes quite hardy in sheltered spots.

The following species are rather taller but admirable for the larger frame and are well worth searching for:

I.aitchisonii, pale and dark lilac-purple or yellow. 30 cm (12 ins).
I.albo-marginata, grey-blue with a yellow patch. 37 cm (15 ins).
I.cyclogossa, shades of true blue with a white crest and large, erect standards. 30-90 cm (1-3 ft).
I.kopetdaghensis, greenish yellow with vestigial standards. 30 cm.
I.stocksii, lilac-purple with a yellow crest. 25-30 cm.
I.vicaria, violet and white with a yellow or white crest. Like a more exotic form of *magnifica*. 30-37 cm.
I.warleyensis, pale violet with deep violet patch and a deep yellow crest. 45 cm (18 ins).

Finally for the devotee there is one of the earliest of the Junos and one of the most exciting, *I.nicolai*. A miniature, about 10 cm (4 ins), it has falls of pale rose-violet with a purple blotch and a golden crest, and standards of slaty-white. It is sweetly scented and grows with vigour. It resembles *I.rosenbachiana* and is a triumph to grow in the bulb frame.

Less well known than they deserve to be, the Junos are specially delightful flowers and we hope that they will one day achieve their rightful place in the spring bulb display.

The Hexapogons

From perhaps the most exquisite of irises we move now to certainly the most exotic. These are of the Hexapogon section, the rather special type of bearded iris which come from the arid mountainous regions of the Near East and Southern Russia. Outstanding among them are the Oncocyclus section. They are distinguished by having single, unbranched stems and very large flowers with broad and rounded, often incurved, falls and standards, heavily veined and dotted and in vivid colours. They grow from short, red-skinned rhizomes with crowded growth and the seeds have white or creamy-white arils which are readily distinguished. They are not easy to flower but with a bulb frame their natural growing conditions can be simulated. Like the Junos they need to be dried off in the summer after flowering and to be kept dry right through to the spring. Any water on them at any time will cause growth to start and this must be controlled so that growth is restricted to the proper season. Most of the many Oncocyclus species will grow well in the frame but a few (to be listed later) need to be kept in the alpine house as they appear to be more winter tender. Among those which are reasonably easy to obtain are:

I.gatesii. Flowers 12 cm (5 ins) wide with a ground colour of pale greenish or grey-white, closely marked with fine purplish veins and dots. 37-60 cm (15-24 ins).

I.ibirica. White or pale yellow, lightly veined standards and very rounded, spoon-shaped falls, very closely stippled and veined in purple brown. 5-20 cm (2-8 ins).

I.lortetii. White standards, finely veined reddish-violet and rounded falls closely dotted in crimson with a central blotch of dark crimson. A superb and stately iris not always frost hardy. 30 cm (12 ins).

I.sari. A shorter variety with many colour variations. Grey, yellow or lavender ground heavily blotched with lilac purple or chestnut-brown. 5-8 cm (2-3 ins).

I.susiana. The largest and the earliest recorded member of the

76

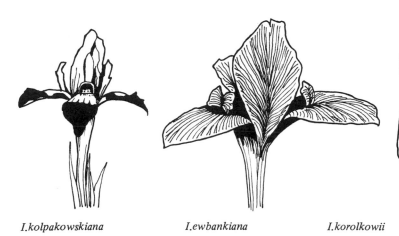

I.kolpakowskiana   *I.ewbankiana*   *I.korolkowii*

family, *I.susiana* was said to have come from Constantinople in 1573 and was named after Susa, the ancient capital of Persia. The distinctive dark purplish colouring is produced by dark purple-black veins and dots on a grey ground. 37 cm (15 ins).

All these can be obtained from Messrs Van Tubergen, famous for the collection and introduction and marketing of irises of this section for a hundred years.

Another group in the Hexapogon section needing special care in the control of watering are the 'sand irises', often classed among the pogon irises and not all that easy to find. Specially suited to the bulb frame and specially rewarding are these small early flowering spring beauties:

I.bloudowii, clear yellow with a golden beard. 15 cm (6 ins).
I.potaninii, named after the Russian traveller Potanin. Yellow or
    purple. 5 cm (2 ins).

Figure 7.4
Iris kolpakowskiana,
Iris ewbankiana and
Iris korolkowii

The other Regelia irises can stand rather more watering than the oncocyclus and psammiris and are not quite so 'difficult'. They also have the advantage of having more than one flower, in fact up to three to a stem. In this group we have what is probably our favourite of all species irises, the incomparable *I.hoogiana*. This truly wondrous plant has flowers of the perfect classic shape, of a pure, soft and unmarked blue at a height of about 50 cm (20 ins). There is also a white form, the flowers being of the palest possible blue-white — quite ethereal. The beard in each case is golden yellow. *I.hoogiana* is ideally grown in the frame or alpine house but it can also do well in a very dry, sunny spot out of doors. It will need to be covered in winter with a sheet of glass fixed at about 25 cm

(10 ins) from the ground. It is worth mentioning that our hero W.R. Dykes recorded having more than a hundred blooms of *I.hoogiana* at one time in open-sided frames in his garden at Godalming. It was growing 'like a weed'! The following are regelia species which are more easily found:

I.afghanica, greenish-cream ground heavily veined in purple-brown. 15-30 cm (6-12 ins).
I.hoogiana, pure clear blue with golden beard. 45-50 cm (18-20 ins).
I.korolkowii, long and pointed flowers with a creamy-white ground veined with green, black or dark purple. 30-36 cm (2 ft-2 ft 2 ins).
I.stolonifera, light or dark brown-purple shot with electric blue. Free-flowering and very decorative. 30-60 cm.

Of the small group of Pseudoregelias distinguished by their sharply pointed flowers and mottled colouring here are two which are reasonably available and look well in the frame:

I.kamaonensis, mottled lilac. 10-15 cm (4-6 ins).
I.hookerana, lilac blue. 13 cm (5 ins).

Regeliocyclus hybrids are also available and are well suited to the bulb frame.

Other Irises for the Frame

Of the more normal bearded irises virtually all the MDB and MTB cultivars are suitable for and look most attractive in the larger frame. There are also a number of species which are not always winter hardy and will benefit from the shelter of the frame:

I.imbricata, BB, yellow. 20-30 cm (8-12 ins).
I.kashmiriana, TB, whitish-lilac. 70 cm (2 ft 4 ins).
I.mellita, MDB, brown-purple. 3 cm (1¼ ins).
I.mesopotamica, TB, red-violet. 95-120 cm (3-4 ft).
I.pseudopumila, MDB, many colour forms. 10-18 cm (4-7 ins).
I.scariosa, MDB, red-purple or yellow. 10-15 cm (4-6 ins).
I.schachtii, SDB, yellow-green, 23 cm (9 ins).
I.subbiflora, SDB, blue-violet. 25 cm (10 ins).

Although not very vigorous out of doors these species will grow very quickly in the shelter of the bulb frame so that care should be taken in the planting not to let them overrun the more delicate types.

Finally for the frame there are one or two individual and unusual species which are exciting to grow and cherish:

I.decora. The best known species in the sub-genus Nepalensis. It grows from a bunch of fleshy roots and has very pretty lilac-blue flowers. It requires plenty of water while in growth. 15-37 cm (6-15 ins).

I.tuberosa, the 'widow iris', green and black scented flowers. 15-30 cm (6-12 ins).

I.sisyrinchium, blue-purple or lilac flowers growing to 30 cm from a corm. Should be planted 2 cm (1 in) deep and treated in the same way as Reticulata.

I.grant-duffii. This is one of the beardless rhizomatous irises of the sub-genus Syriaciae, rather difficult to find. It has yellow flowers. 15-25 cm (6-10 ins). Best grown in a frame.

I.minutoaurea, a tiny species of the series Chinensis. Yellow. 10 cm (4 ins).

Finally, to search for and grow as a curiosity if you can is *I.tenui-folia* — another tiny iris with blue-purple flowers.

If the bulb frame is large enough the more robust crested irises will give bloom later in the year and are magnificent in their handsome branching and delicate, frilly flowers. The species suggested are:

I.confusa, pure white with an orange crest. 30-95 cm (2-3 ft).
I.formosana, white, ruffled with a white crest. 20-37 cm (8-15 ins).
I.japonica, pale lilac with an orange blotch. 30-45 cm (12-18 ins).

The Alpine House

All the irises which have been described in this chapter will grow well in the alpine house, either in pots or in a bench bed with undersoil watering. The *reticulatas* are best grown in pans in a mixture of John Innes Compost or soilless compost and 'pea' grit or broken bricks (not dust). The bulbs should be planted in the autumn at a depth of 2 cm (1 in). The Junos and hexapogons are best planted in deep pots 'Long Toms', set inside pans filled with sandy soil and watered in the pans only. They like a mixture of John Innes Compost and 'pea' grit.

In addition to the smaller Junos already mentioned there are a number which are more tender and must be frost-free. They are well worth searching for for the alpine house. Their ephemeral beauty is very special and they will amply reward the care they require:

I.baldschuanica, a delicious creamy-white form of rosenbachiana. 10 cm (4 ins).
I.cabulica, a real miniature. Lilac or near-white. 3 cm (1¼ ins).

I.doabensis, early flowering. Yellow. 0-15 cm (-6 ins).

I.palaestina, an ethereal beauty with almost transparent greenish grey-white flowers. 0-7 cm (-3 ins).

I.planifolia (formerly known as *alata*), one of the earliest flowering of the group. Blue or white. 0-30 cm (-12 ins).

I.popovii, blue-violet. 0-10 cm (-4 ins).

I.rosenbachiana, perhaps the most popular. Pale mauve or whitish with purple falls and an orange ridge. 0-10 cm.

I.zaprjagajevii, unpronounceable maybe, but a charming miniature white. 5 cm (2 ins).

In addition we would specially recommend for pot growing in the alpine house *I.caucasica*, *I.persica* and, of course, the most delectable *I.nicolai*.

A lot of the Oncocyclus section are rather tender and really need the frost-free conditions of the alpine house. They are difficult to obtain, but we list them here for reference and they are more fully described in the classification. *I.antilibanotica*, *I.atrofusca*, *I.atropurpurea*, *I.bismarckiana*, *I.haynei*, *I.heylandiana*, *I.jordana*, *I.lortetii*, *I.nigricans*, *I.petrana* and *I.samariae*. As already mentioned, *I.lortetii* is worth trying in a frame if well sheltered.

Other species for the specialist to try in the greenhouse are these three from the Evansia section:

I.pseudorossii, blue-white and purple-blue. A very rare and beautiful flower. 8-14 cm (3-6 ins).

I.speculatrix, another rarity in this country. A collector's item from Hong Kong. Pale lilac-blue with a purple patch and an orange crest, all on a rather long, slender stem. 23 cm (9 ins).

I.wattii, a tall species with flowers similar to but larger than those of *I.japonica*. Lilac with an orange crest. 90-120 cm (2 ft 11 ins-4 ft).

These are all heavy feeders and grow best in a gritty compost with well-rotted manure added. They should be mulched in the spring and autumn with a mixture of soilless compost and grit.

CHAPTER 8

Irises as Cut Flowers

The irises most commonly used as cut flowers are those of the Xiphium sub-genus and in particular those known as Dutch irises. These are not true species but a race produced in the early 1900s by the Hoog Brothers of the Van Tubergen firm in Holland. They were hybrids of *I.xiphium*, the Spanish iris, and other species and are finer in form and substance than the true species. The variety most widely used in commerce and to be seen in most florists' shops is the pale blue 'Wedgewood'. This was raised by the old-established Dutch firm, de Graaff Brothers, and in 1926 became the only bulbous iris to receive the First Class Certificate of the Royal Horticultural Society.

Dutch irises normally flower out of doors in the late spring but they can be forced to provide blooms from Christmas time almost throughout the year. The normal bulbs obtainable commercially should be planted in the late autumn, about 8 cm (3 ins) deep in a well-drained bed. Most of them will show growth before the winter and in very severe weather the tips of the leaves may be browned but they will not normally be killed.

Bulbs are supplied wholesale in three sizes. The ones usually available from nurserymen are known as 'good flowering size' of which about 75 per cent can be expected to flower. The next size up are 'strong bulbs', which will produce about 95 per cent flowers, while the final grading is 'top size' or 'largest selected', likely to give 99-100 per cent flowering. These are obviously the ones to opt for if a choice is available.

It is also now possible to buy 'retarded' bulbs for flowering in the late summer or autumn. These bulbs have been specially treated by heat storage followed by controlled cold storage. It may happen that the treatment has not been quite correct and the bulbs may fail to flower and be blind. They can, however, be planted again in a rich compost and should be satisfactory for following years. The new bulbs they produce will flower at the normal time or they may possibly miss a year.

When cutting the flowers it is best to leave as much foliage as possible on the plant. The flowers should be cut when the first bud is about to open and they will last well in water with the other buds opening in the normal way. After flowering and when the foliage has died down the bulbs can be dug up, dried, cleaned and stored for re-use. In a really hot, dry situation the bulbs may be left in to form clumps. Dutch irises are normally available in named varieties of which the best are:

'Wedgewood', of course, the pale blue;
'White Perfection', a splendid pure white;
'Professor Blaaw', a good deep blue;
'Purple Sensation', a dazzling flower of deep purple and gold.

Spanish irises are similar to the Dutch but they have smaller bulbs and they flower some three weeks later on taller, rather thin stems. They have been developed from generations of collected forms of *I.xiphium*. They usually come in shades of yellow, bronze and purple, are offered as mixed varieties and are splendid as cut flowers.

English irises are similarly most useful for cutting since they flower even later than the others, in mid-summer. They are descendants of *L.latifolia* (for long known as *I.xiphioides*) which was native of the alpine meadows of the Pyrenees. Brought to England by seafarers, they were first appreciated by gardeners when seen growing in the Bristol area and became known as 'English' irises. They like a rich soil and moist, cool conditions and prefer not to be disturbed. They come in white and shades of blue and purple and are usually sold as mixed varieties.

I.tuberosa

Another iris most attractive as a cut flower is the so-called 'widow iris' or 'snake's head iris', *I.tuberosa* (*Hermodactylus tuberosa*). Commonly grown commercially in Cornwall and the Scilly Isles, these are usually available in the better-class florists' shops. The pale-green flowers with their dramatic black blotch are often lost when grown in the garden but come brilliantly alive in a vase. They are also very sweetly scented. In cultivation they like a hot, dry situation but tend to be a little 'choosy'. If they fail in one position they are quite likely to do well in a new spot near at hand.

I.unguicularis

Another wonderful iris, useful for cutting, which can be temperamental is our beloved *I.unguicularis*, the winter-flowering Algerian iris. Sidney Linnegar writes of it:

> It was one of the first irises I ever bought, at the age of 12, and after receiving it in spring from a well-known mail-order firm, I planted it in an open sunny spot where it grew and grew and

Figure 8.1
I.unguicularis
(Winter-flowering
Algerian Iris)

never flowered. Three years later I borrowed my father's barrow and lifted the plant in one piece, nearly a barrow full, and struggled with it to the front of the house where I dumped it on top of the ground by a low south wall. Although the house gave it shade for most of the day and it was never planted, but simply had soil thrown around the roots, it at once began to flower.

The species owes its name (Poiret, 1785) to the narrowness of the base of the segments of the flowers, unguiculus being the Latin for a narrow finger-nail or claw. Its more pleasant-sounding name, *stylosa*, was given to it later in 1798 by Desfontaines because of its typical long style.

The common Algerian form has narrow leaves, 30-50 cm (12-20 ins) long, and the flowers tend to remain low in the foliage. Blooming in the winter months, they can be easily damaged by the weather, by slugs or even by mice, so they are best if cut when in bud and brought indoors. There they can be seen to open in the warmth of the house and will last for several days, remaining fresh and clean and exquisitely beautiful. The colour of the flowers varies a good deal from pale to deep lavender with faint veining. A most beautiful and unique feature is that the backs of the style branches have the appearance of being sprinkled with gold dust. The time of flowering also varies, very much influenced by the weather. After a hot, dry summer the flowers are usually abundant and will appear as early as October, while after a damp, sunless season there may be no flowers until February.

There are two additional species: *I.lazica*, from the shores of the Black Sea, which has dark, blue-purple flowers which grow very low in rather prolific foliage, and *I.cretensis*, from Crete and Asia Minor, which has smaller, heavily veined blue and gold flowers. There are a number of varieties of *I.unguicularis*, mostly unnamed, including a delicate white form which tends to flower later and is smaller, less robust and less floriferous. The finest two varieties were collected by E.B. Anderson outside Algiers in 1962. 'Mary Barnard' is a deep shade of lilac and a fine grower; 'Walter Butt' is very vigorous and early flowering with large flowers of the palest lavender with deep green markings. All varieties are sweetly scented.

The typical Algerian variety is best grown close up against a sunny wall in soil which has lime rubble mixed with it. We have seen *I.unguicularis* flowering vigorously when planted between two hedges and we conclude that the siting does not matter so long as the soil is right. The best time for planting is the early autumn. *I.unguicularis* really likes to be left alone but if it has to be moved, it should be divided into good-sized clumps and not reduced to single rhizomes. After being moved it may very well sulk for a few years, but rest assured it will flower again in its own good time.

These lovely *stylosas* (as we like to call them) are among the most delightful of all cut flowers. Arranged either singly, in a tiny glass vase, in groups in low bowls or mixed with Forsythia or the winter Jasmine they bring joy at a time when few other plants are in bloom.

Other Irises for Cutting

We have mentioned the irises which are at their best as cut flowers but most irises can be used with advantage in floral art, and we will comment on those which last longest and seem to fit in best. In the late spring the Pacific Coast, or Californian irises are specially attractive for use as table centre pieces. These and their many hybrids in a wide range of colours blend well together and have the special exotic quality associated with small orchids. The Siberians also make lovely, elegant blue-and-white arrangements though they are not very long lasting. Our native *I.pseudacorus* lasts very well in water and is splendid when mixed with the blue-purple *I.versicolor*. The individual flowers of the 'yellow flag' are short lived and need tidying up daily, but the buds will open in water in their normal sequence.

The Louisiana irises are quite superb as cut flowers. Their fine branching gives them a special elegance; the flowers are graceful in themselves and come in many colours and the buds will continue to open on the stems for as many as six or seven days.

The Spurias as a whole are also admirable for cutting. Most popular is *I.orientalis* (*ochroleuca*) which is best used to give a massed effect. *I.monnieri* and *I.spuria* are equally useful as background flowers in large arrangements. The Spuria hybrids, looking like giant Dutch irises, last well in water and are magnificent when used for large-scale displays. The stems and leaves are perhaps a little heavy for normal use and it is well to remember that the nectar tends to drip from the top of the stems. Where space is restricted the lovely, scented *I.graminea* and *I.kerneriana* are two delicate species well worth using for decoration.

Equally delicate in appearance are the elegant evansias, the Japanese crested irises with their slender, branched stems and small, lacy flowers. They give an orchid-like appearance to an arrangement but need daily attention for the removal of the dead flowers. It should be noted that such species as *I.confusa*, *I.formosana*, *I.wattii* and *I.japonica* and the newer hybrids will root in water. They can, therefore, be used for decoration in water and at the same time roots will form and new stock be obtained. Charcoal should be put in the water to keep it sweet and the stems should be potted up when the roots appear.

Contrary to common belief the tall bearded irises are quite splendid for use as cut flowers. There is surely nothing more wonderful than a mass of TBs arranged in a tall vase standing in the hall or the fireplace. The irises are best cut just as they are coming into flower and they will open beautifully and last well indoors. For smaller rooms the MTBs come into their own as their many buds give a long display. The smaller bearded irises have only a limited use indoors and are perhaps best left in their natural setting outside.

For winter dried arrangements the seed pods of many of the species irises are very attractive, and specially for use are the Spurias, Sibiricas and Chrysographes. The pods of *I.pseudacorus* are much sought after and, of course, the very special *I.foetidissima*. This plant produces strangely shaped seed pods, which, when they dry and break open, reveal strings of brilliant red seeds which have the unusual quality of adhering to the pods and will last through the winter.

The Japanese irises (Hanashubu), described in Chapter 4, are lovely when used as cut flowers and have been widely used in Japan for many centuries for decorative and ceremonial purposes. They are best used in simple, elegant arrangements in a watery setting to display to advantage the spectacular blossoms.

With their varied and graceful forms and wonderful range of harmonious colours, irises are ideal for use in floral decoration.

They can be used in many ways, according to taste, but we feel that they are probably best on their own in simple arrangements rather than mixed with other plants, so that the beauty of the individual flowers can be appreciated to the full. A point worth making and so often overlooked by flower arrangers is that, when used as cut flowers, irises require a specially adequate supply of water. For arrangements for special occasions, such as flower shows, not required to last very long, small containers filled with 'oasis' can be used but care must be taken to see that this does not dry out. For arrangements for the house, required to last for a week or more, containers should be used which will ensure plenty of water all the time.

Indoor Plants

Many of the smaller irises may be grown as indoor plants and of the bearded irises, the MDBs, SDBs and even the IBs can be potted up and will do well in a sunny position. Most useful, however, for this application are the small bulbous Reticulatas. For the best results the bulbs should be planted in October in a large trough in a mixture of soilless compost and 'pea' grit with a generous application of 'Phostrogen' or 'Seagold'. The trough should stand in a cold frame, covered in heavy frost. When the buds appear the bulbs can be lifted and planted in suitable indoor pots and taken into the house to flower. The pots or pans are best if they have drainage holes. By using the mixture described the bulbs can be lifted and transplanted without harm. When flowering is over they can be replanted outside and will flower the following year if given liquid feed until the leaves die down.

Also eminently suitable for growing indoors is the graceful *I.japonica*. Set against a darkish background the branching stems with many star-like flowers are very attractive and the plants will revel in central heating.

Window Boxes

For window-box culture only the smaller irises requiring dry conditions are recommended. Here again the small bulbous Reticulatas are most suitable, followed by the MDBs, SDBs and IBs and finally the MTBs. More exotic effects can be obtained by using the regelio-cyclus hybrids and the smaller arilbred irises. They can be grown in the way described for pan culture of the Reticulatas. It is best to have a special set of window boxes for irises so that they can be left in them for years and put on show when the flowers appear. With proper care the bearded irises can be left for two or three years before replanting in fresh compost. The Reticulatas will also keep going but it is really best to have fresh bulbs each year. For them it is specially important to have the boxes thoroughly cleaned each year to reduce the risk of ink spot disease which attacks them and for which there is no cure except clean husbandry.

CHAPTER 9

Iris Societies, Shows and Showing

The delight in growing irises can be much enhanced by being shared with others who have similar interests. Throughout the world there are iris societies dedicated to the spreading of knowledge and interest in this loveliest of flowers. They originally date back to the period just after the First World War, when there was an explosion of interest in gardening in general and in irises in particular. The advent of such exciting new varieties as 'Dominion' and the other Bliss TB seedlings and of the revolutionary French raisings such as 'Alcazar' and 'Ambassadeur' swept iris growers off their feet and a whole new iris world came into being. This resulted in the foundation of both the American and the British Iris Societies.

The British Iris Society

The British Iris Society was founded in 1922 by a group of enthusiasts led by W.R. Dykes and since then has devoted itself to the 'encouragement, improvement and extension of the knowledge and cultivation of irises'. The range of its activities is wide. It holds shows for all classes of irises; it conducts garden trials of new irises, giving to them a series of awards which lead to the Premier Award, The Dykes Medal; it issues literature in two forms, standard booklets on cultivation, etc. and the *Year Book* and periodical newsletters to keep information up to date. The *Year Book* is universally regarded as the finest of such publications and the series dating from 1924 constitutes an unrivalled treasure house of iris knowledge. The Society maintains a lending library and a slide library. It operates a seed-distribution scheme and a plant-sales scheme which enables members in the United Kingdom to obtain a wide range of classic and modern irises not otherwise available. It works closely with the Royal Horticultural Society in connection with their trials and award scheme.

Associated with the Society are a number of specialist and regional groups. The Species Group caters for those particularly interested in species irises, publishes detailed information about them and holds regular meetings and plant sales. Also for the specialist are the Remontant Group and the Siberian, Spuria and Japanese Iris Group. Regionally, the Mercia Group covers the area north west of London, the Kent Group covers the area south east of London, the West Midlands group is for members further to the north and the Avon Group for those in the west country. The Groups are friendly, intimate organisations holding meetings and arranging their own shows and outings and so on. They are noted, it may be said, for the outstanding quality of their teas.

The American Iris Society

The American Iris Society is the largest of the societies, reflecting the enormous interest in irises in the USA. It was founded in 1920, largely at the instigation of that great irisarian, John C. Wister. It has produced a series of great works on the genus *Iris*, the latest of which, *The World of Irises*, published in 1978, is a comprehensive and valuable monograph. It also publishes quarterly bulletins with up-to-date information. The Society is responsible for the registration and naming of all new irises and publishes an annual list of such registrations with a consolidated list every ten years. The Society's Annual Convention is the Mecca for all iris lovers. It conducts garden trials and gives awards for all classes of iris with the Premier Award also of the Dykes Medal, presented annually by the British Iris Society.

Other Societies

Active iris societies flourish in almost every part of the world and there is a constant interchange of news and information between them. They all feature wonderful iris shows and, of these, we should perhaps mention especially the great Iris Competition in Florence. This is organised annually by the Italian Iris Society in collaboration with the City of Florence. Irises submitted are grown in the Iris Garden at the Piazzale Michelangelo and of the many awards given, the Premio Firenze, the 'Gold Florin', is among the most coveted in the iris world.

We do most strongly recommend that anyone interested in irises should join a society or group. This is the great way of increasing one's knowledge and of improving one's collection of irises. It is also the way to meet the nice people associated with the iris. We list below the principal iris societies and groups with the names and addresses of their secretaries.

The British Iris Society.　　　　G.E. Cassidy,
　　　　　　　　　　　　　　　67 Bushwood Road,
　　　　　　　　　　　　　　　Kew, Richmond,
　　　　　　　　　　　　　　　Surrey, TW9 3BG.

Species Group.　　　　　　　　Prof. M.E.A. Bowley,
　　　　　　　　　　　　　　　Brook Orchard, Graffham,
　　　　　　　　　　　　　　　nr Petworth, Sussex.

Remontant Group.	H. Drayton, 112 Barclay Rd, Edmonton, London, N18 1EQ.
Siberian, Spuria and Japanese Group.	Mrs G.J. Trevithick, 86a Grantham Road, Radcliffe-On-Trent, Nottingham.
Mercia Group.	Mrs E.M. Wise, 197 The Parkway, Iver Heath, Iver, Bucks.
Kent Group.	Mrs R.S. Tubbs, 9 Lingfield Road, Wimbledon Common, London, SW19.
West Midlands Group.	Mrs J. Hewitt, Haygarth, Cleeton St Mary, Cleobury Mortimer, Kidderminster, Worcs.
Avon Group.	C.E.C. Bartlett, Somerset College of Agriculture, Cannington, Bridgwater, Somerset.
The American Iris Society.	Mrs Carol H. Ramsey, 6518 Beachy Avenue, Wichita, KS, 67206, USA.
The Canadian Iris Society.	Mrs Alberta Richardson, R.R.2. Hannon, Ontario, Canada.
Gesellschaft der Staudenfreunde.	Herr Herman Hald, 7250 Leonberg bei Stuttgart, Justinus-Kernerstr. 11. Germany.
The Iris Society of Australia.	C/o R. Raabe, P.O. Box 22, Wentworthville, NSW 2145, Australia.

The Iris Society of Southern Africa.	P.O. Box 82, Bedfordview, Transvaal, RSA.
The Japanese Iris Society.	17 Kitamomodani, Minami-Ku, Osaka City, Japan.
The New Zealand Iris Society.	Mrs H.E. Collins, R.D.1. Cambridge Rd., Tauranga, New Zealand.
Societa Italiana dell'Iris.	The Secretary, Palazzo Strozzi, Florence, Italy.
Société Françaises des Iris et Plantes Bulbeuses.	Mme Helene Muzard, 6 Rue Villaret de Joyeuse, 75017, Paris, France.

The other splendid way of increasing one's knowledge of, and adding to one's pleasure in irises is to take part in the iris shows. This we recommend in the strongest possible terms. Showing is the greatest fun and the important thing, as with the Olympic Games, is not the winning of prizes but the taking part.

Iris Shows

The British Iris Society holds shows for the various classes of iris at the appropriate times, a Reticulata Show in the early spring, a Dwarf Show in the late spring and then the summer shows for the tall bearded and other species. There is also a decorative show in mid-spring and classes for decorative arrangements at all the shows. The regional groups also hold their own shows locally so there is no lack of opportunity for having a go.

Growing for Show

The main objective in preparing plants for showing is, of course, to have them at their peak of perfection on the day of the show. This is by no means easy to achieve as we are all at the mercy of the weather. It is perhaps a little less difficult in the case of the smaller irises which can be grown in pots or pans for the early shows. For the Reticulatas the process begins in the late autumn when the fresh bulbs are planted in pots or pans in a loam-free compost mixed with an equal amount of 'pea' grit with a heavy feeding of 'Seagold' or 'Phostrogen'. They are watered-in and left out of doors or in a cold frame over the winter. About six weeks before the show date they can be brought into a warmed greenhouse and slightly forced. If, nearer the date of the show, they require more forcing it is advisable to apply heat very gradually otherwise the bulbs can grow 'blind' and fail to flower. At the same time as increasing the heat it is desirable to increase the length of daylight by using artificial light. Suitable lamps are available commercially of the mercury filament type and a 400-watt lamp hung 75 cm (2 ft 6 ins) above the plants will cover an area of 1.25 m (13 sq.ft). These lamps should not be used in a living room or where one would work under them for long periods.

Perhaps the best way of really bringing on the flowers in a very late season would be to keep them in a heated fish tank (without water, of course) with a strip light over the top. About twelve hours with a bright daylight lamp should bring the bulbs into flower. As the buds appear they need to be watched very carefully and the plants may need to be put outside in a cool place to keep them back. This 'in and out' process may need to be done several times. At this stage, just before the show, the plants can be repotted to provide the correct number of bulbs required in a pot or pan by the show schedule. The compost and grit mixture will allow the bulbs to be lifted and the roots disentangled without breaking and they can be easily repotted.

For dwarf bearded irises similar procedures can be adopted. If those which are grown in open ground are very backward they can be potted up about four weeks before the show and forced in the same way as the Reticulatas. If flowers alone are required for showing and not the whole plant, an old-fashioned 'bell jar' can be placed over the clump in the garden.

Juno irises for showing can be grown singly by using 'growers' pots — No. 4 'Long Toms'. These are pots 10 cm (4 ins) in diameter but with the extra depth of 12 cm (5 ins) which allows the thick roots to develop. They should be grown as already described in Chapter 7.

Growing tall bearded irises for showing is much more a matter of chance and the luck of the weather, since for the amateur gardener the forcing or holding back of these irises is not really a practical proposition. Commercial growers, with greenhouses of different temperatures at their disposal can achieve a degree of control. Their irises are planted singly in pots, using John Innes No. 1 Compost and heavily fed. Carefully watched, they can be moved from one house to another and made to flower at exactly the right time. We understand that the late Harry Randall used to hire his local butcher's deep freeze to keep back irises for late shows and gained many wins with flowers which had been stored hanging on meat hooks! For the rest of us it is a matter of getting to know which irises will do well at the right time and it is wise to grow early, medium and late-flowering varieties.

Obviously extra care should be taken in the garden with spikes which are likely to be suitable for showing. Although we are not generally in favour of staking, exceptional spikes should be carefully staked and tied. Care must be taken not to damage the buds with the stakes and they should be tied in at each branch base and each branch should be supported.

If the weather is bad a few days before a show, stems which look promising may be cut and put into a bucket of water, taking care to keep them upright and not touching. When the buds are dry and about one-third open, plastic chrysanthemum caps can be put on them. These must not be pulled down to the tops of the flowers but left with a 3-4-cm space at the top. If the weather is dry the stems should be cut on the morning of the day before the show and the caps put on. The aim should be to arrive at the show in the evening before the first day or as early as possible on the day of the show, when the caps should be removed.

Transporting Irises

Transporting irises is a difficult business since they are obviously so delicate and can be so easily damaged. Much care and ingenuity are required to keep the flowers in perfect condition in transit to shows.

For Reticulatas and dwarf irises in 15-cm (6 in) pans use can be made of the polystyrene containers used for packing 4 x 1-litre chemical bottles. The clay pans will fit snugly into the holes, supported by their rims, but plastic pans will need supporting from below. The centre hole can be used for a jar of cut blooms.

Figure 9.1
Transporting Irises

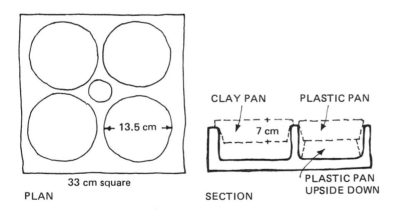

CLAY PAN   PLASTIC PAN

13.5 cm

7 cm

33 cm square

PLAN

SECTION

PLASTIC PAN
UPSIDE DOWN

The method of packing and carrying tall bearded irises depends very much on the type of transport available. With a van or a large estate car deep buckets can be used, taking care to pack the stems firmly so that they remain upright and are not touching. In a small

93

estate car or in a fair-sized boot, racks can be made of wood or metal and the irises laid horizontally on them and tied to prevent movement. For other means of transport it is best to use a large strong cardboard box such as those used commercially for carnations. If buds are beginning to open the stems should be raised above the bottom of the box with rolls of paper or corrugated cardboard and the stems must be supported along their length. If the stems are reversed for the next layer and so on, up to four layers may be carried in one box. If all the buds are capped the stems may be packed in the box using thick layers of tissue paper.

At the Show

When arriving at the show, unpack the stems carefully, remove the chrysanthemum caps and place the stems in buckets or vases, wedging them upright and putting more than one stem in a vase. Always remember that there are other exhibitors and that at most shows, space is valuable. So do not take more than your fair share of the vases supplied and do not take more than your fair share of staging space. Fill each vase one-third to a half full of water and place a stem in the centre. Pack around the stem with a rolled-up piece of newspaper kept above the level of the water. Dry newspaper used thus will keep the stem in position while soggy paper will only make more work for the show committee when clearing up. Top up the vase with green tissue or moss, clean the vase, take it to the appropriate place on the show bench and label the exhibit. Half-open flowers can be persuaded to open fully by blowing on them gently or a clean, soft paint brush can be used to ease them open. Flowers which have opened just before judging are not usually fully expanded or as fresh looking as those opened for about an hour.

Before planning and staging exhibits it is most important to READ THE SCHEDULE carefully and comply with its conditions. The correct number and kind of spikes or plants stipulated must be shown otherwise the entry will very sadly be marked 'NAS' (Not according to schedule).

If a collection of irises is required by the schedule a good selection of colours should be shown and it is best not to put two spikes of the same variety next to one another. If, for example, a collection of blue irises is called for, the whole range of colours should be included rather than a predominance of light or dark shades, e.g. 'Blue Sapphire' 'Eleanor's Pride' 'Pacific Panorama' 'Shipshape' 'Allegiance' 'Arabi Pasha'.

If you are in any doubt on any point regarding the show, ask the Show Secretary who will give you guidance. Never be shy of seeking help from a more experienced exhibitor — it will always be forthcoming.

Figure 9.2
Displaying Irises

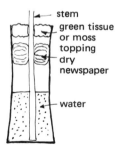

stem
green tissue
or moss
topping
dry
newspaper

water

Finally, if you do not win a class always remember that it is those who don't always win but who enter for the fun of the thing who really make a show. If only perfect and winning irises were entered there would be very little to look at. However, as we all like to do our best, here are some judging criteria as a guide:

Good Exhibit	Bad Exhibit
Stem straight.	Stem with kink.
Well-spread branches.	No branching or bunched.
Three or more flowers open.	One flower going over and one forced open.
Clean break where first flower has been removed.	Half seed pod left where first flower removed.
Clean foliage.	Spotty foliage.
Clean flowers.	Bruised or torn flowers.
Clean vase.	Dirty vase. (When provided chipped this should not count against the exhibitor).
Stem well supported.	Stem loose in vase and untidy finish.
Well-printed label. (If name is not known mark 'name unknown').	No name or other information.

CHAPTER 10

Advanced Iris Fever

Hybridising

One of the many delightful features of members of the iris family is that they pollinate easily, set seed readily and can be grown from seed without great difficulty. It is small wonder, therefore, that many iris-lovers, once firmly caught by the iris 'bug', are moved to try their hands at hybridising. This can be the greatest fun and a most interesting hobby. It is a natural human urge to want to produce something new and better and in growing iris seedlings there is no knowing that something really new and wonderful may not result. Who knows — even a Dykes Medal winner may emerge and there is no harm in dreaming. It is a surprising fact that many of the best modern irises have been raised by amateurs rather than by the professional breeders. Though the best of these have usually come from hybridisers giving much time and study to genetics, none the less many really good varieties have come from less knowledgeable amateur raisers.

For hybridising it is not, therefore, essential to know all about chromosomes, genes etc., but a basic knowledge of them does lead to a better understanding of the mechanics of fertilisation. Irises have two sets of chromosomes in every cell. These chromosomes contain genes which determine the characteristics of the plant, how it grows and reacts to disease, the size, form and colour of the flowers, the spread of its branches and the number of buds and how it will stand up to garden conditions. The flower contains both the male organ (stamen) and the female organ (ovary). When the flower is open these have half the chromosomes (not by number but by being split down the middle). When the pollen from a stamen is put on the stigma of another flower the pollen grows down into the ovary and unites with an ovule which also has only half the chromosomes. When they are fused together they start dividing into cells to form the seed and the new combination of genes produces a slightly or very different plant when the seeds have germinated.

The process of fertilisation, therefore, involves the transfer of pollen from the stamen of one flower to the stigma of another. This process is carried out in nature by the wind or by bees or other insects and the flowers are designed especially to make this possible but prevent self fertilisation. Beardless irises are more frequently pollinated by bees than the TBs. This is because they have a com-

Pacific coast 'Blue Ballerina'

Tall bearded 'Tangerine Sunrise'

Tall bearded 'Olympic Torch'

I. tectorum

Regeliocyclus 'Dardanus'

I. laevigata alba

Tall bearded 'Dominion'

Oncocyclus *I. lortetii*

I. hoogiana

Tall bearded 'Rippling Waters'

Sibirica 'Wisley White'

I. pseudacorus

Dwarf bearded 'Melon Honey'

I. magnifica

Dwarf bearded 'Eyebright'

Irises in a small garden

Tall bearded 'Dachstein'

I. foetidissima

Cal-sib 'First Down'

Reticulata 'Cantab'

paratively small 'tunnel' (see Chapter 1) whereas the TBs have a larger 'tunnel' and small insects can reach the nectar without brushing the stigma or even the stamen. Only the large bumble bees are likely to carry pollen from one flower to another on their backs.

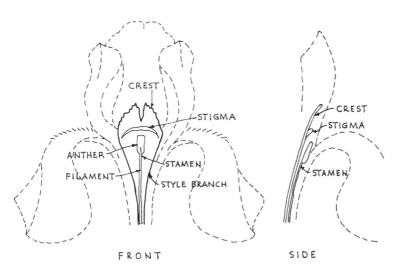

Figure 10.1
Diagram showing
the Reproductive
Parts of the Iris

FRONT   SIDE

A simple method of hand pollination is as follows. Remove the petals from the flower which is to bear the seed. With a pair of tweezers remove the stamen from the plant selected as the male or pollen parent. The stamen must have split open and have pollen grains showing which can be pale blue, white or pale or deep yellow. With your free hand lift the top of the style crest under which is the stigma which should have a wet, sticky appearance (Do not touch to see!). Then gently pull the stamen on the stigma and pollen grains should be left behind. It is a good idea to do this to all three stigmas although one is really sufficient. This method may seem a little wasteful of pollen but it does save having to wash and dry paint brushes or whatever implements are used.

For those who wish to delve more deeply into the mysteries of iris genetics we recommend: *Iris Culture and Hybridizing for Everyone* by Wilma Vallette (1961) (which can be borrowed from the British Iris Society library) and *The World of Irises* (1978) published by the American Iris Society. There are also many books on genetics and general hybridising which should be available through local libraries.

In hybridising irises, as in any form of breeding, the choice of parents is the most important factor. For the beginner this must be based on personal taste, advice from the more experienced, 'hunch' or luck. The expert will draw on experience and scientific rules of inheritance and compatibility. There are two general avenues of approach, the first of which is known as 'line breeding'. In this case the parents are chosen from irises of similar colour and form, breeding on with other irises of similar colour and bringing in other parents only slightly different. In this way can be produced a 'line' of irises of roughly one colour and form, but improving with each generation. As an example there was the classic line of blue varieties which came originally from 'Great Lakes' (itself a child of 'Dominion') which, crossed with 'Missouri' produced 'Chivalry'. Thence, through 'Violet Harmony' came 'Cloud Castle' which, crossed with 'Purissima' gave 'Helen McGregor'. Thereafter the line continued through 'Seathwaite' and 'Patterdale' and, with the introduction of 'Jane Phillips', eventually to 'Eleanor's Pride'. Line breeding does not, however, always work just like that. For example, in the 1940s, Sir Cedric Morris was producing a fine line of Plicata irises in the famous 'Benton' range when there suddenly emerged from two Plicata seedlings the first true pink self – 'Edward Windsor'. From this breakthrough was developed a great line of pink irises culminating in the memorable 'Benton Cordelia'. So you can never tell what will happen.

The second approach is to cross irises of different forms and colours in the hope of combining their special qualities. The results are usually referred to as 'out crosses'. We quote two famous and successful examples. Hugh Miller's splendid white 'Kangchenjunga' Dykes Medal winner in 1960, was a cross between 'Desert Song' (yellow) and 'Jane Phillips' (blue). Leonard Brummitt's 'Primrose Drift', a lovely yellow self (Dykes Medal 1964) came from 'Arabi Pasha' (deep blue) and 'Cosmetic' (peach/apricot). It is beyond our scope to go more deeply into the subject of breeding, but beginners will find good reading on the subject in *The Iris* by N.L. Cave and *The Iris Book* by Molly Price.

Because of their universal appeal the tall bearded irises have tended to dominate the iris world, and it is in this field that most hybridising is carried out, and many hundreds of varieties are introduced each year. There is, however, much scope for improvement in the smaller bearded irises and we hope for news of an extension of breeding in these, especially the miniature tall bearded for which there should be space in every garden. While hybridising of the iris species is limited, there is scope for much interesting work. In the bulbous group hybrids of the Reticulatas have been made, but rarely, and they deserve more attention. Sections which are regularly used for crossing are the Sibiricas, Californians, Louisianas and Spurias with some lovely resulting varieties while in Japan there are many superb hybrids of the Japanese irises. Interesting hybrids, though usually sterile, can be produced from Pogoniris x *tectorum*, Chrysographes group x Californian group and the Dutch iris x Spuria though the latter are not always successful. Further development within the Chrysographes group is to be encouraged while the use of *I.setosa* with the Siberian group requires further investigation. There is scope for experiment in crossing *I.pseudacorus* with *versicolor/laevigata* and *ensata* (*kaempferi*) and there are exciting reports from Japan of yellow Japanese irises developed in this way. In the Juno group it is felt that first generation crosses should result in plants easier to grow as shown by the ancient but very lovely 'Sindpers' (*sindjarensis* x *persica*). Similar improvements are seen in the Regeliocyclus (Regelio x Oncocyclus) and the modern aril hybrids.

In the species field there is clearly room for vast improvement in the future and we would like to see the development of varieties of all the species which are easier for the average gardener to grow. As to the future of the tall bearded irises, we view with some horror the popularity of 'curiosities' with horns and spoons and much too heavy frilling. We prefer the smooth or very slightly waved irises, with wide-flaring or semi-flaring falls and well-domed standards.

Iris seed is best sown as soon as it is ripe. It has been found that in six months old seed germination is rather slower but seed stored for 7-10 years usually germinates quite well. Longer than that we cannot tell, but Sir Michael Foster is said to have sown seed of Oncocyclus which germinated fifteen years later.

Growing from Seed

Seeds may be sown in open ground, in a cold frame or in pots. Where space permits a cold frame is probably best, left open and, if necessary, protected from mice with a fine mesh. When sowing outside or in a frame, prepare the ground by digging a spit deep, incorporating bone meal at a good handful per square metre and sand to help drainage if the area is likely to become waterlogged. Rake down the soil to remove coarse stones and leave a good tilth. Then gently firm the ground with the back of a rake, not too much but enough to compress any extra large air pockets. Sow the seeds about 1 cm (½ in) deep in straight rows, leaving at least 20 cm (8 ins) between the rows and between types if more than one are put into a row. Keep a plan showing where the different types are sown so that if the labels get moved they can still be traced. For growing seeds in pots it is best to use 'Long Toms' with Levington soilless compost mixed with 'pea' grit in equal parts. The pots should be 75 per cent filled, leaving plenty of room for expansion as soilless compost expands in the frost much more than does John Innes compost. The pots should be plunged into the ground so that the level of the compost is just above soil level. (Figure 10.2)

Frost does not harm the seed and in fact, after frost, seeds seem

Figure 10.2
Growing Irises
from Seed

 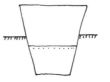 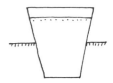

Good.
Excess water can
drain away.

Poor.
Compost becomes
waterlogged and
seeds will rot.

Poor.
Compost will expand
above rim of pot and
seeds can be lost.

to germinate much better. If some early-ripening seed germinates before frost it will come to no harm if it is not too wet. If, however, general germination is good before frost and the seeds are in pots then the best place thereafter is the cold frame. One or two raisers are now using another method of germinating TB iris seed. The seeds are thoroughly soaked in, preferably, sterilised water and the skins peeled off completely. They are then placed in batches, by cross, into small freezer bags with a handful of moistened peat or vermiculite and put into the lowest compartment of a refrigerator. After three or four months at a temperature of 2°C. they develop shoots up to 8 cm (3 ins) long and can be planted in seed boxes and grown on in a cool greenhouse. With this method there are some problems with rot, but the rate of germination is very high and the seedlings are many weeks in advance of normal development.

Embryo
Culture

For the slower germinating species such as the Hexapogons and the Hexapogon/Pogon hybrids the growing of embryos in an agar medium is practised. The seed is usually soaked in deionized water for 2-3 days and the skins removed. With a very sharp scalpel the growing shoot is removed, put in a petrifying dish with an agar and sugar mixture and kept in a dark place for four days. Then they are removed into a warm, light (not bright) spot and when the roots and shoots have developed they are potted in sterilised compost in very small pots. They are then transplanted as the pots become root bound.

Tissue Culture

This is a method of producing plants from the growing tip without any, or very little, vascular system. It is used under laboratory conditions to produce virus-free plants and though the method is simple enough it takes time, care and space. It is hardly for the amateur, but the Dutch have produced virus-free strains of 'Wedge-

100

wood' and 'Imperator' and work on some TBs is being done at the Glasshouse Crops Research Institute, Rustington.

Seedlings should be transplanted at the three-leaf stage. If the soilless compost/'pea' grit mixture is used they can be carefully shaken out without too much damage to the root system. With the grown seedlings removed the pots should be plunged again and left for another year (even longer for arils) to see if more seed will germinate. Transplanting

The seedlings are best planted in rows, which makes it easier to mark the crosses or species, 25 cm (10 ins) or 50 cm (20 ins) apart, dependent on whether they are robust (TBs) or less robust, such as MDBs. The distance between the rows should be at least 75 cm (2 ft 6 ins). When the plants have flowered any that are poor and weak should be discarded. Those to be retained and grown for another year should be numbered and a description kept for reference.

Unless an iris is outstandingly different it should be tried out in as many positions as possible before being considered for naming. It is quite possible to have a splendid iris which will grow happily in only one spot. For example, Alec Howe's 'Aurelian', a very good iris for bud-count, branching, colour and flower form, would grow well only on its home allotment and at Wisley. Elsewhere it often failed to flower and was, therefore, not a good garden plant.

At all stages of the raising process it is essential to label all plants and keep accurate records. At the first stage the seed bearing plant should have a label showing the identity of both parents. A 'stud' book should be kept containing details of all crosses with dates, etc. Seedlings which show promise are usually given a raiser's number and it is the usual practice to give an iris a name only after it has been selected for trial. To be eligible for competition an iris must be registered and have its name approved. The American Iris Society is the body responsible for the registration of irises all over the world and in the United Kingdom the British Iris Society acts as its agent. Application forms for registration may be obtained from the British Iris Society's Registrar.

The naming of irises, like the naming of racehorses, is becoming very difficult and calls for much ingenuity to avoid duplication. General and confusing names such as 'the first' or 'the best red' are not now allowed. Simple and relevant names are, of course, desirable and some hybridisers adopt a personal prefix such as Sir Cedric Morris's 'Benton Pearl' etc. and Mrs Brummitt's 'Banbury Beauty', and this is a satisfactory solution.

Our Favourite Irises

	Sidney Linnegar	George Cassidy
MDB	Orchid Flare Bee Wings Knick Knack	Blue Pigmy Dunlin Joanna Taylor
SDB	Cherry Garden Gingerbread Man Widecombe Fair	Amphora Small Wonder Widecombe Fair
IB	Kiss Me Kate Cutie Piona	Brighteyes Chiltern Gold Indeed
MTB	New Idea Ice Fairy Peewee	New Idea
BB	Lace Valentine Junior Prom Frenchi	Pink Ruffles Tulare
TB	Ola Kala Allegiance Blue-eyed Brunette	Marshlander Starshine Jill Rosalind
Aril	Grand Vizier Saffron Jewel Promise	Lady Mohr Dardanus Grand Vizier
Louisiana	Black Widow Clyde Redmond G.W. Holleyman	
Sibirica	Nottingham Lace Cambridge Orville Fay	Cool Spring Caesar's Brother Canonbury Belle
Spuria	Elixir Connoisseur Morningtide	Academus Morningtide Shelford Giant
California	Banbury Beauty No Name	Banbury Beauty Banbury Candy

	Native Warrior	Arnold Sunrise
Japanese	Numazu	
	Stranger in Paradise	
	Star at Midnight	
Evansia	Bourne Graceful	Bourne Graceful
	Queen's Grace	Bourne Noble
	Bourne Noble	
Reticulata	Katherine Hodgkin	Katherine Hodgkin
	Harmony	Hercules
	Violet Beauty	Pauline
Dutch	Purple Sensation	Purple Sensation
	Professor Blaauw	Professor Blaauw
	Symphony	White Perfection
Regeliocyclus	Barcarolle	Vera
	Vera	
Cal/Sib	Margot Holmes	Margot Holmes
Other	Holden Clough	Holden Clough
Species	*I.aphylla*	*I.bucharica*
	I.bucharica	*I.chrysographes*
	I.chrysographes	*I.delavayi*
	I.chrysophylla	*I.fulva*
	I.foetidissima	*I.histrioides*
	variegata	*I.hoogiana*
	I.fulva	*I.imbricata*
	I.gatesii	*I.lactea*
	I.gracilipes	*I.lutescens*
	I.graminea	*I.magnifica*
	I.histrioides	*I.nicolai*
	I.hoogiana	*I.tectorum*
	I.iberica	*I.unguicularis*
	I.lactea	
	I.japonica variegata	
	I.kernerana	
	I.latifolia	
	I.lortetii	
	I.mellita	
	I.nicolai	
	I.pallida variegata	
	I.pamphylica	
	I.persica	
	I.pseudacorus	
	variegata	

I.setosa (dwarf)
I.tectorum
I.unguicularis

I cannot forbear to mention that during the preparation of this book I spent a month in hospital in mid-winter and not a day passed without my wife bringing me buds of *I.unguicularis* to make life more bearable. I shall be forgiven for saying that it is without doubt my favourite iris and, indeed, my favourite flower.

G.E.C.

A Selection of American Tall Bearded Irises

This list has been prepared by one of our leading growers, Mr Jack Venner, and all the irises named have grown and flowered for him for at least two seasons. They are recommended as suitable as garden plants for the United Kingdom. The names of the raisers and the dates of registration are shown in parentheses.

'Sapphire Hills' (Schreiner 71)
The bluest mid-blue, with large flared and gently ruffled flowers.

'Chapeau' (Babson 69)
Semi-flared with creamy standards and bluish-mauve falls.

'Fresno Calypso' (Weiler 78)
Deep orange with large flaring flowers. Vigorous and well branched.

'Western Hostess' (Babson 77)
Lavender-blue and a superbly vigorous grower.

'Shipshape' (Babson 68)
Deep Oxford blue with flaring flowers gently ruffled. Dykes Medal winner.

'Dream Lover' (Tams 70)
Lilac-pink standards and deep-purple falls. A splendid Dykes Medal winner.

'Chamber Music' (Williamson 72)
A giant bi-colour with tan-brown standards and violet and brown falls with orange beard.

'Homeward Bound' (Nearpass 76)
A refined iris with flared and ruffled flowers, peach standards and pale violet falls.

'Love Theme' (C. Benson 70)
Well-shaped flowers of a deep shade of pink.

'Pink Angel' (Rudolph 72)
A quality iris in a glistening shade of pale pink with a pink beard.

'Golden Brilliance' (Mahlestein 73)
A vigorous deep yellow self.

'Entourage' (Ghio 77)
A spectacular and exotic iris — a mixture of salmon, beige and lilac-mauve. Very floriferous.

'Peek-a-Blue' (Sexton 75)
A white and blue plicata with semi-flaring flowers.

'Flare Up' (Ghio 77)
A good dark brown with lighter falls.

'Repartee' (K. Smith 66)
Cream standards and red-brown falls.

105

'Going My Way' (Gibson 71)	A magnificent white and black-purple picotee-plicata.
'Irish Spring' (Roe 72)	A lovely iris, mainly white but with a faint green flush on the semi-flaring falls.
'Wedding Vow' (Ghio 70)	A very fine white, well branched and flared.
'Royal Trumpeter' (Reynolds 72)	Maroon-red with ruffled flowers on well-branched stems.
'Mission Ridge' (Plough 72)	A superb near amoena mostly white with violet-blue on the falls.
'Bayberry Candle' (De Forest 66)	A curious mixture of yellow and olive with a hint of green — semi-flared.
'Countryman' (Gaulter 75)	A grand yellow with white spot under the beard — broad flaring falls.
'Sun King' (Stahly 77)	Very striking combination of cream, white and yellow.
'Heavenly Harmony' (Hamblen 78)	Beautifully ruffled with pink standards, violet falls and a red-orange beard.
'Evening Echo' (Hamblen 77)	Very tall with striking flowers, pale French-blue with a dark-blue beard.

Mr Venner also recommends two Australian varieties:

'Alpine Sunshine' (Blyth 75)	Ruffled lemon-yellow and white amoena.
'Jovian Magic' (Blyth 76)	Tall with pink flowers overlaid bluish-mauve.

Buying and Acclimatising Irises from Overseas

When buying and having irises sent from overseas it is important to ensure that they are free of soil, disease and pests, and they must have a Health Certificate issued by the appropriate Government Health Department. This certificate must be on the outside of the parcel. Parcels without the certificate displayed are not usually opened and by the time a duplicate certificate is obtained much valuable time will have been lost.

When the dried-out rhizomes are unpacked the roots should be wrapped in sphagnum moss, put to soak with water up to the base of the rhizomes and left in a cool, dark place for 48 hours. They should then be removed from the water, excess moisture shaken off and the whole ball that is left potted up in John Innes compost. Our favourite soilless compost dries out too much for this purpose.

If plants come from other hemispheres they are best put into a cold frame or greenhouse, otherwise they can be left in the open and planted in spring. Plants from Europe and the USA will normally flower in the first year, though they may be stunted, but those from the other hemisphere may well take up to two or three years to settle down.

Doctor Iris
(Pests and Diseases)

Clean cultivation with good, friable soil is better than any chemicals, but pests and diseases do occur and here is a list as a guide with symptoms and controls.

PESTS

Pest	Symptoms	Control
Stem Eelworm (*Anguillulina dipsachi*)	Bulbs have yellow streaks on outer scales. Brown and black patches when bulbs are cut transversely. Foliage chlorotic. English and Dutch Irises (Wedgewood and Imperator types)	Dip in Thionozin as a protection, not a cure. Burn infected bulbs and sterilise soil. Bulbs treated with hot-water are usually clear.
Root Knot Eelworm (*A.meloidogyne*) and Strawberry Eelworm (*Aphelenchoides fragariae*)	Swollen root tips. Sometimes leaves become distorted by a thickening of veins.	Burn, or hot-water treatment and sterilise area where grown. Drench with Thionozin. (Protection not cure).

(Hot-water treatment: Bulbs: as soon as ripe immerse for 1-2 hours at 43°C (109°F). Rhizomes: immerse in solution of 1 part 38% formaldehyde to 200 parts water for 30-40 mins at 52°C (126°F.)

Pest	Symptoms	Control
Bulb Mites (*Rhizoglyphus echinopus*)	Usually attached to bulbs and rhizomes that have been damaged.	Drench or dip in Thionozin.
Grey Field Slug (*Agriolimax agrestis*)	Foliage clawed, usually by young slugs. Stems attacked by adult slugs.	Put down slug pellets. Water late at night or at dawn with liquid 'Slugit', or
Black Field Slug (*Arion hortensis*) (*Milax sowerbi*) Underground	Foliage clawed. Rhizomes hollowed out. Bulbs chewed.	trap in ground with orange peel, potato etc. Must be inspected daily and slugs destroyed.

108

Foliage rasped.	Water with liquid 'Slugit' or put down bait.	Snails (*Helix aspersa*)
Bulbs and rhizomes eaten often following attacks by slugs and wire-worms.	Treat with HCL dust (Lindane) or naphthalene, 90 grams (3 oz) per sq. metre.	Millipedes (*Blanjulus guttulatus* and *Polydesmus complanatus*)
Note: Never use Lindane near potato crops.		
Flowers eaten by larvae. Often the ends of the flowers of *I.unguicularis* in a warm, sheltered spot.	Spray with derris, pyrethrum or HCH.	Angleshades Moth Larvae (*Phlogophora meticulosa*)
Flowers and foliage infested with green-fly.	Spray with derris.	Aphids (*Myzus circumflexus, Aphis newtoni, Anuraphis tulipae*)
Bulbs and rhizomes infested with green-fly.	Dip in nico-soap or pyrethrum dust.	
Flowers with clean cut holes.	Dust with nicotine or spray with nico-soap.	Blossom Beetles (*Meligethes viridiscens* or *Euparia aestisa*)
Flowering stems eaten, usually at night. Stems of reticulata section and Dutch and English irises.	Trap in jam jars. Dust with pyrethrum dust.	Cockroaches (*Blatta orientalis* or *Periplaneta americana*)
Foliage rasped, mostly on waterside plantings. Not usually in sufficient numbers to warrant control. Care must be taken not to harm fish in ponds with spray.	Dust or spray with HCL.	Donacia Beetles (*D.semicuprea, D.sericea, D.simplex*)
Pin holes in leaves. Young leaves may be notched. 'Sawdust' at base of plants in summer. Hollowed-out rhizomes.	Dust or spray with HCL.	Iris Borer (*Macronoctua onusta*) Not yet found in UK
Holes in flowers and damage to seed pods. Mostly in beardless irises, sibirica and chrysographes sections and *versicolor*.	Dust or spray with HCL.	Iris Snout Beetle or Iris Weevil (*Mononychus vulpeculus*) Not yet found in UK
Foliage mined. *I.foetidissima*, *I.pseudacorus* and Spuria series.	Best to remove and burn leaves attacked. Malathion may control.	Leaf Miners (*Agromyzadizygomyia iraeos*) (*A.lateralla* not in UK)

109

Leatherjackets (Wireworms) (*Agriotes obscurus*)	Roots and rhizomes eaten.	HCL dust forked into soil around plants.
Sawfly Larvae (*Rhadinoceraea micans*)	Foliage with edges eaten. Usually only attacks *I.pseudacorus*. (Keep spray and dust from fish in ponds)	Nicotine dust or nico-soap.
Swift Moth Larvae (*Hapialus lupulinus*)	Attacks bulbs, rhizomes and roots. Rhizomes with large cavities.	Fork in naphthalene, 60 grams per sq. metre (2 ozs per sq.yd.)
Thrips (*Bregmatothrips iridis*)	Russeting or blackening of foliage. Flowers 'bloated'.	Spray with malathion.
Verbena Bud Moth (*Endothenia Nebesana*)	Small holes in seed pods.	Burn infected capsules.
Vine Weevil (*Otiorrnynchus sulcatus*)	Roots eaten. Bulbs and rhizomes tunnelled.	Fork-in HCL dust.

DISEASES

Blossom Blight (*Botrytis cinerea*) and (*Glomerella cingulata*)	Wet grey spots on buds, petals and sometimes stems of bearded irises. Cinnamon-red zonate spots on flowers of Xiphium group.	Thiram.
Bulb Rot (*Penicillium* spp. *Fusarium oxysporum*, *Sclerotium rolfsii*)	Develops quickly in stored bulbs. Bulbs feel soft and when scale leaves removed rot spreads from base of bulbs.	Burn infected bulbs. Dip before storing in Maneb as a preventive.
Crown Rot (*Sclerotium rolfsii*) White Bulb Rot (*S.delphinii*)	Bearded, Japanese, sibiricae, spuria, evansia and bulbs. Leaves yellow at top and rot at base. Leaf topple. Bulbs white and soft.	Drench with Thiram or Orthocide.
Ink Disease (*Mystrosporium adustum*)	Mostly reticulatas but can infect other bulbous irises. Black crusty spots or streaks on bulbs of reticulatae. Black	Remove and burn. Sterilise ground before replanting.

streaks on new leaves of Xiphium which die before maturing.

Large irregular spots running between 'veins' of leaves. First wet-looking and brown. Bad only in very wet seasons. Rhizomatous irises only.	No known control. Cut off infected leaves and burn. Clean cultivation is a preventive.	Leaf Blight (*Xanthomonas tardicrescens*)
Small black spots on leaves of rhizomatous irises.	Spray with Maneb or Zineb.	Leaf Spot (*Didymellina macrospora*)
Plants wilt and fail to flower.	Drench with Thiran or Zineb.	Oak Root Fungus (*Armillaria mellea*)
Black mould in rhizomes. Leaves do not grow. Rhizomes become leathery.	Cut out infected areas and drench with Thiram.	Rhizome Rot (*Sclerotina convulata*)
Damping off of iris seedlings.	Water pots with Zenal. Before sowing water with Orthocide.	Root Rot (*Rhizoctonia solani* and *Phytophthora*)
Small oval or oblong yellowish spots.	Spraying with Zineb will control spread but will not kill infected parts.	Rust (*Puccinia iridis, P. sessilis*)
Infected rhizomes smell like 'bad eggs'. Leaves wilt and turn yellow and plant dies.	Cut out infected areas of rhizome and burn. Dry off plant before replanting. Drench with Thiram.	Soft Rot (*Erwinia caratovora*)

VIRUSES (Transmitted by aphids or by the use of infected tools, such as pruning knives)

Mottling of flowers and leaves. Blindness in bulbs. Colour breaking.	Dig up and burn.	Iris Mosaics MIMV (Bulbous) SIMV
Flowers deformed and puckered. Leaves thickened. Some show hardly any symptoms.	Burn badly infected plants.	BIMV (Rhizoma-tous)

There is no practical cure for virus diseases, the symptoms of which are more apparent after cool, wet weather in the autumn and spring. Work is being done towards the production of virus-free plants and bulbs, so far successful in the case of some varieties of Dutch iris.

Blindness	Bulbous irises fail to flower.	Often due to wrong storage conditions. No control.
Pineappling (Not in UK)	Rhizomes enlarged. Leaves dwarf. Stems malformed.	No control. Burn.
Scorch	Central leaves wither, turn red-brown. Roots die. May be due to soil condition and amount of lime. If the infected plant is a very special one, it may be dug up and replanted 15 cm (6 ins) deep in very well-drained soil in a greenhouse. It may develop and form new rhizomes under the surface and flower after two or three years.	No control. Dig up and burn.

Iris Suppliers

Jacques Amand, Beethoven Street, London, W10 4LG.	Dutch, Japanese, species.	United Kingdom
Avon Bulbs, Bathford, Bath, BA1 8ED.	Bulbous, oncocyclus, species.	
Walter Blom & Sons Ltd, Leavesden, Watford, Herts, WD2 7BH.	Bulbous.	
Bressingham Gardens, Diss, Norfolk, IP22 2AB.	Species and water irises.	
Broadleigh Gardens, Barr House, Bishops Hull, Taunton, TA4 1AE.	Small bulbous, Californian, regelia, species.	
Groom Bros. Ltd, Claylake, Spalding, Lincs.	Bulbous.	
V.H. Humphrey, 8 Howbeck Road, Arnold, Nottingham, NG5 8AD.	Dwarf and intermediate bearded, species and water irises.	
W.E.Th. Ingwersen Ltd, Birch Farm Nursery, Gravetye, East Grinstead, Sussex, RH19 4LE.	Species.	
P. de Jager and Sons Ltd, The Nurseries, Marden, Kent, TN12 9BP.	Tall and dwarf bearded, species.	
Kelways Nurseries, Langport, Somerset, TA10 9SL.	Tall, intermediate and dwarf bearded, bulbous and species.	
R.C. Nottcutt Ltd, Woodbridge, Suffolk.	Tall bearded, species.	
J. Parker Dutch Bulbs Co., 452 Chester Road, Manchester, M16 9HL.	Bulbous.	

J. and E. Parker-Jervis,   Species.
Marten's Hall Farm, Longworth,
Abingdon, Oxon. OX13 5EP.

Robinson's Hardy Plants Ltd,   Species.
Greencourt Nurseries,
Crocken Hill, Swanley, Kent.

Sunningdale Nurseries Ltd,   Bearded, species.
Windlesham, Surrey.

Van Tubergen Ltd,   Bulbous, species.
P.O. Box 156,
Kingston-upon-Thames, KT2 6AN.

The nurserymen listed stock only a small range of species irises. Occasionally species may be found in local nurseries and it is very much a case of 'shopping around'. Species may be obtained by members of the Species Group at their regular plant sales.

A wide range of classic and modern bearded irises, which are not available from nurserymen, can be obtained through the British Iris Society's plant-sales scheme.

Overseas

Melrose Gardens,   Wide range of bearded, Remon-
309 Best Road, South, Stockton, tant, Arilbred, Spuria, Louisiana,
Ca. 95206. USA.   Siberian, Japanese and water
                              irises.

Cordon Bleu Farms,   Bearded, Arilbred, Spuria, Louisi-
418 Buena Creek Road,   ana, Siberian and Pacific Coast.
San Marcos, Ca. 92069. USA.

Laurie's Garden,   Bearded, Spuria, Louisiana,
17225 McKenzie Hwy, Rt.2.,   Siberian, Pacific Coast, Japanese,
Springfield, Or. 97477, USA.   Cal. Sib. and beardless species
                              and hybrids.

Riverdale Iris Gardens,   Wide range of dwarf and inter-
7124 Riverdale Road,   mediate bearded and species.
Minneapolis, Minnesota,
55430, USA.

Miller's Manor Gardens,   Good range of bearded varieties
P.O. Box 105, Markle, In.   and bearded species.
46770, USA.

Schreiner's Gardens,   Wide range of bearded, Spuria
3625 Quinaby Road, Salem,   and Siberian.
Or. 97303, USA.

Tira Nurseries,   Oncocyclus species and hybrids.
Tirat, TSVI, Doar NA,
Emek Beit Shean,
10815, Israel.

There are many more nurserymen in the USA and in other parts of the world offering a wide range of irises, and we list only those of which we have personal knowledge.

A Classification of the Genus Iris

MORE FOR THE GARDENER THAN THE BOTANIST

Botanically the genus Iris can be divided into 10 sub-genera (numbered from 1 to 10), which subdivide into 19 sections (shown in capitals (A), (B) etc.), 24 sub-sections (shown in roman numerals) and 59 groups or series (shown in small letters (a), (b) etc.). These groups require similar cultivation so it is helpful for gardeners to know to which group each iris belongs.

Genus Iris	Sub-genus	Section	Sub-section	Group or series
	1. *Iris*	(A) Pogoniris	(I) Eupogon	(a) Miniature dwarf bearded. (MDB)
				(b) Standard dwarf bearded. (SDB)
				(c) Intermediate bearded. (IB)
				(d) Miniature tall bearded. (MTB)
				(e) Border bearded. (BB)
				(f) Standard tall bearded. (TB)
		(B) Hexapogon	(I) Regelia	(a) Regelia
				(b) Falicifolia
				(c) Psammiris
			(II) Pseudoregelia	
			(III) Oncocyclus	(a) Acutiloba group
				(b) Iberica group
				(c) Sari group
				(d) Polakii group
				(e) Susiana group
				(f) Atropurpurea group
				(g) Haynei group
				(h) Ungrouped
	2. *Crossiris*	(A) Evansia	(I) Evansia	(a) Japonicae
				(b) Tectores
		(B) Lophiris	–	Cristatae
		(C) Monospathae		
	3. *Limniris*	(A) Limniris	(I) Apogon	(a) Sibiricae
				(b) Chrysographes
				(c) Prismatica
				(d) Californicae
				(e) Tripetalae

Sub-genus	Section	Sub-section	Group or series
			(f) Longipetalae
			(g) Chinensis
			(h) Laevigatae
			(i) Kaempferi
			(j) Virginicae
			(k) Hexagonae
			(l) Vernae
		(II) Erimiris	(a) Ensata
		(III) Tenuifoliae	(a) Tenuifoliae
			(b) Ventricosae
		(IV) Syriacae	
	(B) Unguiculares		
	(C) Ioniris	(I) Ruthenicae	
	(D) Xyridion	(I) Xyridion	(a) Spuriae
			(b) Gramineae
	(E) Spathula	(I) Foetidissima	
4. *Nepalensis*			
5. *Pardanthopsis*			
6. *Xiphium*			
7. *Iridodictyum*		(I) Reticulatae	(a) Reticulatae
			(b) Monlepsis
8. *Scorpiris*	(A) Juno		
	(B) Physocaulon		(a) Drepanophyllae
			(b) Rosenbachianae
	(C) Acanthospora		
9. *Gynandriris*			
10. *Hermodactylus*			

Other groups to evolve through hybridising are:

Arilbred: hybrids between the hexapogon and pogoniris sections, often marked like the hexapogon but usually branched. Cultural requirements as for pogoniris.

Regiocyclus: hybrids between regelia and oncocyclus sub-sections. Easier to grow but still needing a well-drained, sunny, rich position. Can be grown successfully in a stone sink or on a dry wall or even a bulb frame.

Evanspogon: hybrids between *tectorum* and bearded irises. Usually sterile but worth trying.

Cal/Sibs: sterile hybrids between the chrysographes and Californian series. They require a sunny, rich border which does not dry out during the growing season.

A descriptive list of the species, arranged in accordance with the above classification, with notes as to habitat, garden application and cultivation.

The Genus Iris

1. Sub-genus Iris

This sub-genus contains the bearded irises grown from rhizomes. It is divided into two sections, pogoniris and hexapogon. The pogoniris are the easiest to grow and the most easily hybridised whereas the hexapogon are very unusual and exotic but are very hard to grow.

(A) Pogoniris. This section is sub-divided into six series. The short ones flower in April and the tall ones in June. Most of them will grow well in well-drained, rich loam in full sun.

(a) *Miniature dwarf bearded* (MDB) There are 18 species and many hybrids in this group. They have one or two flowers on stems up to 20 cm (8 ins) with the flowers above the leaves. They are the first of the bearded irises to flower. They are ideal for the rock garden or dry wall, are less robust than the others in this section and must never become waterlogged. They may be moved and divided from the end of July to March.

I.alexeenkoi Gross (1950). Caucasus, Baku province. Single blue flower with yellow beard. 20 cm (8 ins) stem.

I.astrachanica Rodionenko (1961). Russia. Possibly a natural hybrid.

I.attica Boiss Heldr (1859). Greece and Jugoslavia. This fine purple or greenish-yellow iris is sometimes classed as a form of *I.pumila*. It is best grown in a bulb frame or deep pot as it is not always hardy. 3 cm (1¼ in) stem.

I.babadagica Rzazade & Gola (1965). Mt Babadag, Transcaucasia. Two purple-violet flowers. Likely to be a form of *I.furcata*. 15-20 cm (6-8 in) stem.

I.balkana Janka (1876). Balkans. One or two brown or red/purple flowers. 15-20-cm stem. A form of *I.reichenbachii*.

I.barthii Prod & Buia (1946). Romania. One or two greenish-yellow flowers with a pale-blue beard. 3-cm (1¼ in) stem. Often listed as a form of *I.pumila*. Needs to be grown in a bulb frame or alpine house.

I.binata Schur (1960). Balkans. Blue-purple and yellow flowers. 15-cm (6 in) stem. Late flowering. Possibly a natural hybrid.

I.bosniaca Beck (1887). Balkans. A sub-species of *I.reichenbachii*.

I.chamaeiris Bert (1837). S. France, N. Italy, E. Spain. Differs from *I.pumila* in having a long stem, 8-20 cm (3-8 ins) and a short perianth tube. Many colour forms, violet, purple, yellow and white. A very good garden species.

I.furcata Bieb (1819). Caucasus, Moldavia, S.W. Ukraine. (SDB?). Has a branched stem, 15 cm (6 ins), with purple flowers not as large as *I.aphylla* (see SDB) but of a better colour.

I.griffithii Baker (1892). E. Afghanistan. Two purple flowers with a white beard. 12-20-cm (5-8 in) stem.

I.mellita Janka (1876). Balkans, N.W. Turkey. One to three flowers with hardly any stem, usually under 5 cm (2 ins). Colours violet, crimson or yellowish. Beard white often tipped pale blue. Not always hardy but will do in a bulb frame or alpine house.

I.pseudopumila Tin (1827). S. and E. Italy, Sicily, Jugoslavia. One flower, violet, purple, yellow, white or lilac. 10-cm (4 in) stem. Does best in a bulb frame.

I.pumila Linn (1753). E. Europe, Balkans, Caucasus, Trans-Caucasus, N.W. Turkey. Usually one flower but some forms have up to three on a very short stem, 1-2 cm (½-1 in). Many different colour forms, with violet-purple dominant. Range from white, yellow, blue, violet to black. Long perianth tube. Used in hybridising to produce the modern dwarf iris.

I.reichenbachii Heuff (1858). N. Greece, Jugoslavia, W. Romania, Bulgaria, S. Hungary. One or two yellow or brownish-purple flowers with a bluish-white beard. 15-20-cm (6-8 in) stem.

I.scariosa Willd (1820). W. Siberia, Soviet C. Asia, Mongolia. Two flowers, lilac, red-purple veined brown-purple or yellow. 5-10-cm (2-8 in) stem. Best in a bulb frame.

I.taurica Lodd (1829). Caucasus, Crimea, S. European Russia. Flowers often pale yellow. 2-5-cm (1-2 in) stem. Not always hardy. Best in a bulb frame.

I.timofejewii Woronov (1924). E. Caucasus. One violet flower with a white beard. 15-cm (6 in) stem.

(b) *Standard Dwarf Bearded* (SDB). There are eight species and many garden hybrids in this group. They are more robust than the MDBs and flower about a fortnight later. The stems are 21-40 cm (8-16 ins) and are often branched. They are good for the rock garden and for the front of the border. They require rich loam and a warm, sunny position. The modern hybrids come from MDB species crossed with STB irises.

I.aphylla Linn (1753). E. Europe, Caucasus, Ukraine, C. Turkey. Three to five purple-violet flowers with a white or bluish beard on a well-branched stem. 15-45 cm (6-18 ins) stem. Sometimes reflowers in the autumn. Used to bring branching into dwarf irises. There are many named collected forms.

I.benacensis Kern (1887). Italy. (Often included as a sub-species of *I.cengialti*). Blue-purple flowers. 30-cm (12 in) stem.

I.italica Parl (1854). S. and E. Europe. Two or three blue-purple flowers. 25-cm (10 in) stem. Close to *I.chamaeiris* but taller and with larger flowers.

I.lutescens Lam (1789). Italy, S. France and N.E. Spain. (Often considered a form of *I.chamaeiris*). Two or three very pale-yellow, scented, flowers. 25-cm stem only occasionally branched.

I.olbiensis Henon (1855). S.E. France. Creamy flowers. 25-cm stem often with a branch. Possibly a branched form of *I.chaemaeiris*.

I.schachtii Markgraf (1957). Turkey, S. of Ankara. Greenish-yellow flowers. 25-cm stem. It appears to be an early flower-ing dwarf form of *I.imbricata*. Best in a bulb frame.

I.subbiflora Brot (1834). Portugal. One or two blue or deep-violet flowers. 25-cm stem. Best in a bulb frame.

I.virescens Redoute (1809). Italy and France. One or two greenish-yellow flowers. 25-cm stem. It is very close to being a form of *I.chamaeiris*.

(c) *Intermediate Bearded* (IB). The irises in this section are taller than the SDBs with 41-70-cm (16 in-2 ft 4 in) stems and flower just after them, although they overlap a good deal. They require a rich soil and a sunny position and are suitable for the border or large rock garden. There are many good hybrids. The six listed below have lost species status and have been reduced to cultivars.

'Albicans' (*I.albicans* Lange 1860). Yemen, Mountains of S. Arabia. (Naturalised around the Mediterranean, Middle East, Mexico and S. America). Three or four white flowers on a branched stem, 38-45 cm (15-18 ins) tall. There is a blue form *I.albicans* var. 'Madonna'.

'Aphylla' (of gardens) (Linn. 1753. ? *I.plicata* Lam. 1789). Flowers white, veined and flushed lilac, 45-70-cm (18 in-2ft 4in) stem. Well branched with many buds.

'Florentina' (*I.florentina* Linn. 1959). Central and W. Italy, Mediterranean Islands. (Naturalised in S. France, N.W. Africa, S. Spain). Four or five fragrant, white-tinted, pale-blue flowers on a 38-45-cm (15-18 in) stem well branched. Was one of the irises cultivated for 'Orris root'. Now 'Germanica' and *I.pallida* are also used. Often thought to be a form of 'Germanica'.

'Germanica' (*I.germanica* Linn. 1753). Naturalised originally in S. Europe, S. and S.W. Asia, now also naturalised in S. USA. Four, sometimes five, purple-blue or violet flowers on a branched 70-cm (2 ft 4 in) stem. Used for not-such-high-quality orris root. Many different varieties and forms have been collected.

'Kashmiriana' (*I.kashmiriana* Baker 1877). Kashmir, Afghanistan, N. Pakistan, Baluchistan. Two or three very fragrant white flowers with yellow beard. 60-cm (24 in) branched stem.

'Kochii' (*I.kochii* Kern 1887). Istria. Four violet-purple flowers with yellow beard on a 45-cm (18 in) branched stem. Sometimes reblooms in the autumn. Often classed as a form of 'Germanica'.

(d) *Miniature Tall Bearded* (MTB). There are eight species and a number of hybrids in this group. Flowering with the tall bearded irises these charming small irises make good rock garden plants. They are not really recommended to be grown with the tall bearded by which they tend to be overpowered. There are a few good hybrids and more would find a welcome place in the small garden. They have small flowers on wiry stems 41-70 cm (16 ins-2 ft 4 ins) tall. They are usually floriferous and well poised on branching stems and give a long flowering period.

I.cengialti Ambrosi (1886). N. Jugoslavia, mountains of N. Italy. Up to six scented, blue-violet flowers. 45-cm (18 in) stem.

I.illyrica Tomm (1875). Dalmatian coast. Up to six blue flowers. 45-cm stem. Could be a small form of *I.pallida*.

I.narcissiflora Diels (1921). Not very well known, yellow, flowering in July. 30-cm (12 in) stem.

I.perrieri Sim (1935). French alps, Savoy. One to three violet-blue flowers. 30-40-cm (12-16 in) stem. Could be a late flowering form of *I.aphylla*.

I.reginae Horvat (1947). Jugoslavia. Up to 9 flowers on a 40-60-cm (16-24 in) stem. Erect white standards flushed lilac. Falls with plum-violet veining on a white ground. Could be a colour variant of *I.variegata*.

I.rudskyi Horvat (1947). Jugoslavia, Macedonia. Up to 7 flowers on a 45-cm (18 in) stem. Yellow standards and lavender falls veined purple. Possibly another variant of *I.variegata*.

I.taochia Lodd (1829). N.E. Turkey. Mostly two and rarely 5 deep-yellow or reddish-purple flowers on a 40-60-cm (16-24 in) stem.

I.variegata Linn (1753). Widely distributed through the Balkans. 7-11 flowers on well-branched stems, 30-50 cm (12-20 ins). Bright yellow standards and very heavily veined falls appearing red-brown. Used in hybridising to produce the modern STB.

(e) *Border Bearded* (BB). There are 5 species in this group and many hybrids. These are associated with the STBs being similar to them but 41-70 cm (16 ins-2 ft 4 ins) tall. They will grow in any good, sunny, dry position, flower with the TBs and do not require staking.

I.albertii Regel (1877). Turkey. Up to nine purple or yellow flowers veined brown on a branched 60-cm (24 in) stem. Some clones will rebloom in the autumn.

I.bartonii Foster (1883). S. Himalayas. Up to five whitish flowers on a 60-cm stem. Not always hardy. Related to *I.kashmiriana* but less tall.

I.belouinii Bois & Corn (1915). N. Central Morocco. Five to seven large and fragrant flowers on a 70-cm (2 ft 4 in) stem. Like *I.germanica* but is tetraploid.

I.imbricata Lindl (1845). Caucasus. Armenia. Up to five greenish-yellow flowers. 60-cm (24 in) stem.

I.junonia Schott & Kotschy (1854). Sicilian Taurus. Up to seven blue-purple flowers veined brown. 45-cm (18 in) stem. Not always hardy and subject to rhizome rot. Could be a small form of *I.mesopotamica*.

(f) *Standard Tall Bearded* (TB). There are eight species and very many hybrids in this group. They have large flowers. 70 cm and over stems, late flowering. These are the most commonly grown irises. They require to be planted in a sunny position in rich, well-drained soil which does not become too waterlogged. There are a number of collected forms and hybrids.

Many garden hybrids are produced each year, some of which

are improvements and some just 'different'. The most sturdy ones will do well in the garden while others are too tall and require staking. Those who show and breed irises will maintain that the time spent staking is worth while, but with so many varieties to choose from, we prefer not to stake unless the variety is an exceptional one.

I.biliotti Foster (1887). N.E. Asia-Minor. Reddish-purple fragrant flowers on a well-branched stem. 90-cm (3 ft) stem. Evergreen foliage.

I.croatica Horvat (1956). N.W. Croatia. Six to eight violet-blue flowers bicoloured. Similar to *I.aphylla* but with larger flowers and greater height. 75-cm (2 ft 6 in) stem.

I.cypriana Foster & Baker (1888). Cyprus. Up to ten fragrant violet flowers on a 100-cm (3 ft 3 in) stem. Not always hardy and susceptible to rhizome rot.

I.kashmiriana Baker (1877). Kashmir, Afghanistan, W. Pakistan. Four to six creamy-white scented flowers on one or two branched stems 75 cm (2 ft 6 ins) tall. Not truly hardy but possibly the parent of the modern tetraploid irises.

I.mesopotamica Dykes (1913). Turkey, Armenia, Cyprus, Levant. Up to nine blue-lilac scented flowers on two to three branched stems 120 cm (3 ft 11 ins) tall.

I.pallida Lam (1789). Central and N.E. Italy, Tyrol, N. and N.W. Jugoslavia, Sicily, Balearic Islands. (Naturalised in Asia Minor, Crimea, Atlas Mountains and the Pyrenees). Up to nine large, scented lilac flowers on well-branched stems 60-90 cm (2-3 ft) tall. Used in hybridising to produce the modern tall bearded irises.

I.trojana Kern (1887). W. and N.W. Turkey and Central Asia. Seven large blue and blue-purple bitoned flowers on strong, well branched stems 70-120 cm (2 ft 4 ins-3 ft 11 ins) tall. Used in hybridising to produce well-branched cultivars.

I.varbossania Maly (1919). Balkans. Three to five violet flowers. 80-cm (2 ft 8 in) stem. Could be a natural hybrid of *I.pallida*.

Collected clones include:
Amas (Foster 1885). Amasia. Form of *germanica*.
Macrantha. Taller than Amas. Tetraploid.
Ricardi. Could be a form of *mesopotamica*.

Collected hybrids include:
Amoena, Squalens, Sambucina.

(B) Hexapogon. The irises of this section are confined to the drier regions of the Middle East. They have short-jointed rhizomes and not many buds to a stem. The seeds have a characteristic aril and they are known as 'aril' irises. They have been used in hybridising, first between the oncocyclus and regelia sub-sections producing the regeliocyclus hybrids which, though still not easy to grow, are more robust than the rest of the section. They are now used in hybridising with pogon irises and a sturdy unusual race of all heights results. These irises will usually grow under similar conditions to the pogon irises.

Sub-section (I) Regelia.

(a) *Regelia.* These irises come from the mountain regions of Iran, Afghanistan and the Altai range. Rhizome with long stolon. More than one flower to a stem. The flowers are narrow falled and usually striated. Best planted in a deep pot in an alpine house, or a deep, raised bed in a bulb frame. Will occasionally grow outside in a raised bed in a sunny, very sheltered, position. Best planted in October. They need a rich mulch containing magnesium limestone in the spring.

I.afghanica Wendelbo (1972). Afghanistan. Two to three flowers on a 15-30-cm (6-12 in) stem. Standards yellow, falls veined purple.

I.darwasica Regel (1884). Bokhara, Turkestan. Two to three flowers on a 30-cm stem. Pale green or brown veined with red and blue-tipped beard.

I.heweri Grey-Wilson & Mathew (1974). Two to three violet-blue flowers on a short stem, 10-15 cm (4-6 ins).

I.hoogiana Dykes (1916). Turkestan. 'The Queen of Irises'. Two or three pure blue flowers with a gold beard on a 45-cm (18 in) stem. There is also a pure-white form. Can be hardy with careful siting.

I.korolkowii Regel (1873). Turkestan and Russia. Different because it has compact rhizomes. Two to three flowers, creamy-white or light purple veined olive-green or dark purple. 30-36 cm (12-14 ins). Later flowering. Many collected forms.

I.kuschkensis Grey-Wilson & Mathew (1973). Two to three blue-brown flowers. 30-35 cm. Early flowering.

I.lineata Foster (1887). Turkestan. Two to three brown-violet flowers. 60-70 cm (2 ft-2 ft 4 ins). Very similar to *darwasica* of which it could be a form.

I.stolonifera Maxim (1880). Bokhara, Turkestan. Two to

three flowers, light or dark brown-purple, shot with a blade of light or deep blue, with usually a blue beard. 30-60 cm (12-24 ins). An exciting iris for its colours but not really showy although well worth growing.

(b) *Falcifolia*. The irises of this group require similar treatment to the regelias but as they come from the desert regions they are best watered from the bottom.

I.falcifolia Bunge (1847). Afghanistan and the Caspian desert. Two purple flowers on a stem 35-50 cm (14-20 ins). Very slender foliage.

I.longiscapa Ledeb (1853). Afghanistan desert. Two purple flowers. 35-50-cm (14-20 in) stem.

(c) *Psammiris*. These sand irises are sometimes included in the pogon group but as they have an aril, seem to belong to the regelia sub-section or even to a sub-section of their own. They need a very sandy, sunny bulb frame. They have a wider distribution than any other arils so, if given winter shelter or even in a selected spot, should grow in a raised bed or rock garden. Can be grown successfully in a dry raised wall sheltered from north and west. They require lime. Old mushroom compost is good mixed as to 75 per cent coarse (not builder's) sand and 25 per cent mushroom compost as this contains lime. Top dress in the early summer and do not let them dry out while growing in the early spring.

I.arenaria Waldst & Kit (1846). Hungary. A western form of *I.humilis* but more hardy.

I.bloudowii Ledeb (1833). Altai region of Russia and Chinese Turkestan. One or two clear-yellow flowers, slightly veined in brown, with a gold beard. 10-15 cm (4-6 ins). Needs careful watering, is best grown in a covered frame but is well worth growing.

I.flavissima Pall (1776). Hungary, Altai regions, S. Siberia. Up to three bright-yellow flowers with an orange beard. 5-10 cm (2-4 ins). Another form of *I.humilis*.

I.humilis Georgi (1775). Hungary. Altai regions, S. Siberia. Up to three bright-yellow flowers with an orange beard. 5-10 cm. Will survive if looked after on a sunny, dry rock scree with sand added.

I.mandschurica Maxim (1880). Manchuria. A form between *I.bloudowii* and *I.humilis*.

I.potaninii Maxim (1880). N.W. China, Tibet. Early flowering with two yellow flowers on a 10-cm (4 in) stem. Hardy in a sheltered place. Well worth growing. Often included in the pseudoregelia sub-section.

Sub-section (II) Pseudoregelia.

The plants of this sub-section are native to the Himalayas and grow at heights of 5,500 m (18,000 ft). The flowers are similar to those of the Himalayan *I.milesii* and they were once called pseudoevansia. They are more like regelia irises except that they flower before the leaves are fully grown. They are best in a large pan in an alpine house or else in a well-drained bulb frame. They will grow outside in a rich, well-drained, sunny position. Can be grown on a dry wall. There are six species in the sub-section:

I.goniocarpa Baker (1876). Sikkim, W. and C. China. Only one purple or white flower mottled darker on a 20-cm (8 in) stem. Growth is more slender than *hookerana*.

I.hookerana Foster (1887). Kashmir, W. Tibet. Two lilac-purple flowers mottled dark purple on a 13-cm (5 in) stem.

I.kamaonensis Wallich (1877). N.W. Yunnan, W. China. Two mottled lilac flowers on a 1-cm (½ in) stem at flowering time which elongates to 10-15 cm (4-6 ins) after flowering.

I.leptophylla Lingelsheim (1922). Mottled blue flowers. 16-25 cm (6-10 ins).

I.sikkimensis Dykes (1908). Sikkim. Two blue or purple mottled flowers on a 10-15-cm stem. It seems to be between *kamaonensis* and *hookerana* except that it has fine growth like *goniocarpa*.

I.tigridia Bunge (1829). Altai regions, Manchuria. A single yellow or blue-purple flower on a 3-9-cm (1¼-3½ in) stem.

Sub-section (III) Oncocyclus.

These unusual irises come from the Middle East and require special treatment. They have shorter rhizomes than the regelias, only one flower to a stem and sickle-shaped leaves. They require a deep, well-drained position in an alpine house or a raised bulb frame and do best with underground deep watering. Unlike the regelias they will start to grow whenever they receive water so must be left dry until early spring. Then they must be watered only to start growth and gradually reduced so that at flowering time they are ready to be dried off. This sub-section requires research for grouping and we have followed Clay Osborne in the American Iris Society's *The World of Irises.*

(a) *Acutiloba group.* (Elongated, narrow pointed petals).

I.acutiloba Meyer (1832). E. Transcaucasus. Grey veined purple-violet with two spots on falls. 15 cm (6 ins). Worth growing.

I.ewbankiana Foster (1901). Turkmenia, N.W. Iran. Cream, veined brown. 15 cm. Early flowering. Form of acutiloba.

I.grossheimi Woronov (1928). Transcaucasus. Wine-red or deep-brown veined purple. Black-brown signal patch on falls. 5-20 cm (2-8 ins).

I.lineolata Grossh (1940). Transcaucasus. Grey veined, purple-violet with one brown-red or yellow signal patch on falls. Otherwise could be a form of *I.acutiloba*. 15 cm.

I.schelkovnikovii Fom (1907). Azerbaidzhan. Scented flowers of buff-brown or lilac. 20 cm.

(b) *Iberica group.* (Large standards and short, spoon-shaped falls).

I.camillae Grossh (1928). Azerbaidzhan. Pale yellow, blue or pale violet-spotted dark violet on falls very variable. 15-20 cm (6-8 ins).

I.iberica Hoffman (1808). Transcaucasus. White or lilac falls heavily spotted and veined brown-purple, blackish signal patch. Standards white or pale yellow, slightly veined. 5-20 cm (2-8 ins).

I.lycotis Woronov (1925). Transcaucasus. White, heavily veined purple-brown. Blackish signal patch on falls. 5-20 cm. Often classed as a sub-species of *I.iberica*.

(c) *Sari group.* (Long, narrow standards and falls).

I.lupina Foster (1887). Central and eastern Turkey. Greenish-yellow or yellow, veined brown-red. Red-purple signal patch on falls. 25-35 cm (10-14 ins).

I.maculata Baker (1876). S.E. Turkey, N.E. Syria. Whitish ground spotted and veined brown-purple. Dark brown signal on falls. 37 cm (15 ins).

I.sari Schott (1876). S. Turkey. Yellow-veined with brown. 5-10 cm (2-4 ins).

(d) *Polakii group.* (Large standards and stumpy falls sharply recurved).

I.barnumae Foster & Baker (1888). E. Turkey, S. and C.

Syria. Red-purple with darker signal on falls. 15-40 cm (6-16 ins).

I.demavendica Bornm (1902). Elburz mountains of N. Iran. Violet-blue with darker signal on falls. 15 cm.

I.mariae Barb (1891). Egypt and Israel. Pinkish-purple bi-colour with brown-black signal on falls. 15 cm.

I.nigricans Dinsm (1933). W. Jordan. White but so veined and stippled as to appear brown-purple. Standards not quite so heavily veined. Black signal on falls. 30 cm (12 ins).

I.petrona Dinsm (1933). Jordan. Black lilac with black signal on falls. 20 cm (8 ins).

I.polakii Stapf (1885). N.W. Iran. Violet falls with deeper signal patch. Standards lilac veined violet. 20-30 cm (8-12 ins).

I.urmiensis Hoog (1900). E. Turkey, N.W. Iran. Yellow with a deeper signal. 15-40 cm (6-16 ins). A very good plant. Often grouped as a sub-species of *I.barnumae*.

(e) *Susiana group*. (Large, more or less globular flowers. Standards and falls in good proportion. Falls slightly tucked in).

I.basaltica Dinsm (1933). W. Syria. White overcast with deep purple veining. Deep purple signal on falls. 37 cm (15 ins). Could be a form of *I.susiana*.

I.bismarckiana Damm (1890). N. Israel. Falls edged yellow-green veined dark brown in centre. Standards pale-blue veined lilac. 30 cm (12 ins).

I.cedretii Dinsm ex Chaud (1972). Lebanon. White, finely dotted in purple-maroon. Dark maroon signal on falls. Up to 40 cm (16 ins).

I.damascena Mouterde (1967). N.W. of Damascus. Falls grey-white, stippled and veined in purple. Signal patch not very noticeable. Standards grey-white minutely spotted purple. 37 cm (15 ins).

I.hermona Dinsm (1933). S.W. Syria. Cream, dotted and veined lilac. Paler standards. 30 cm.

I.kirkwoodii Chaud (1972). N.W. Syria. Falls greenish-white dotted and veined purple. Standards very pale blue veined blue-purple. Up to 75 cm (2 ft 6 ins).

I.sofarana Foster (1899). Lebanon. White spotted and veined purple. 37 cm (15 ins). Often classed as a sub-species of *I.susiana*.

I.susiana Linn (1753). Probably Lebanon. Greyish-white veined deep purple. Velvety-black signal on falls. 37 cm. A beauty well worth growing.

I.westii Dinsm (1933). Lebanon. Yellow ground, spotted and veined lilac. 37 cm (15 ins). Also often classed as a sub-species of *I.susiana*.

I.yebrudii Dinsm (1972). W. Syria. Falls yellowish-white finely dotted and veined brown-purple with dark purple signal. Standards white dotted purple. 37 cm.

(f) *Atropurpurea group*. (Medium-sized flowers with large standards and falls).

I.antilibanotica Dinsm (1933). W. Syria, E. Lebanon. Purple falls only veined deeper purple with small darker signal. Standards slightly paler. 23 cm (9 ins).

I.atropurpurea Baker (1889). Egypt, Israel. Purplish-black falls with deeper signal patch shading to greenish-yellow. Standards slightly paler. 15 cm (6 ins).

I.auranitica Dinsm (1933). S.W. Syria. Bronze yellow flowers, the falls stippled red-brown with a maroon signal patch. 30 cm (12 ins).

I.bostrensis Mouterde (1954). S.W. Syria. Purplish with dots and veins in red-purple. 35 cm (14 ins). Sometimes classed as a taller form of *I.atropurpurea*.

(g) *Haynei group*. (Long standards and falls nearly as long but recurved so that they look much smaller than the standards).

I.atrofusca Baker (1894). W. Jordan. Dark purple-brown falls with blackish signal. Standards slightly paler. 25 cm (10 ins).

I.haynei Baker (1876). Israel. Falls shading from deep brown at edge to intense black signal. Standards blue-purple with silver sheen. 25-40 cm (10-14 ins).

I.jordana Dinsm (1933). Jordan valley. Falls white densely lined maroon with a deep red-purple signal patch. Standards white and thickly stippled purple. 37 cm (15 ins).

(h) *Species not yet grouped.*

I.elizabethae Siehe (1905). Turkey. Yellow flowers heavily veined purple-brown with a purple-red signal patch on the falls. 15-20 cm (6-8 ins).

I.gatesii Foster (1890). S.E. Turkey. Flowers whitish-lilac spotted and veined greyish-brown with a brown-purple signal on the falls. 37-60 cm (15-24 ins).

I.kasruwana Dinsm (1933). Lebanon. Falls cream dotted and veined dark purple with darker signal patch. Standards white finely lined and dotted purple.

I.lortetii Barb (1882). Israel, Lebanon. Lead-grey falls stippled maroon with brownish-red signal patch. White standards veined deep pink. 30 cm (12 ins).

I.meda Stapf (1885). W. Iran. Flowers yellowish, creamy or whitish-lilac, veined and edged brownish-lilac with a brown-purple signal patch on the falls. 20 cm (8 ins).

I.paradoxa Steven (1844). E. Turkey, Transcaucasus, N.W. Iran. Very small falls edged whitish-stippled pale purple. Large standards white or purple veined darker purple. 15-25 cm (6-10 ins).

I.samariae Dinsm (1933). Israel, Jordan. Cream grounded falls lined and dotted purple, standards cream-lined deep pink. 37 cm (15 ins).

2. Sub-genus Crossiris (The crested irises)

This sub-genus is divided into three sections, evansia, covering the far Eastern crested species, lophiris, including the tiny American crested irises and monospathae, with the one species, *I.gracilipes*.

2 (A) Evansia.

Sub-section (I) *Evansia*

(a) *Japonicae*. In this series are the lovely cane-bearing species from China, Taiwan, Korea and Yunnan. They are not always hardy and are best grown in a cool greenhouse, being too tall for most garden frames. They require very rich, well-drained soil.

I.confusa Sealy (1937). Szechuan, Yunnan. Well-branched cane stem with many white flowers with yellow/orange crest in the spring. The stems are some 25-30 cm (10-12 ins) tall with leaf fans with the flowers at the top of the canes. The leaves tend to flop. Will flower in a warm, dry, sheltered spot outside but not always hardy.

I.formosana Owhi (1934). Taiwan. Not as tall and robust as *I.confusa* this has white, blushed-blue flowers on a branched spike from a 10-15 cm (4-6 ins) cane the overall flower height being 75-100 cm (2 ft 6 ins-3 ft 3 ins). Not hardy.

I.japonica Thunb (1794). China and Korea. Many pale lavender flowers, marked with violet and blotched orange, are carried on well-branched stems 100 cm tall. The leaves are at ground level on short canes in the form of green rhizomes. Ledger's Variety is hardy in a warm, sheltered spot.

I.speculatrix Hance (1875). Hong Kong. A delightful lavender flower blotched with violet and with an orange patch on a 30-cm (12 in) stem. Not many branches and often only two flowers. Leaves up to 25 cm (10 ins). This is the iris which grows nearest to the tropics, is very tender and prefers semi-shade.

I.wattii Baker (1886). Assam, S.W. China. The tallest of all irises and often grows to more than 2 metres (6 ft 6 ins). Many lilac-blue flowers.

(b) *Tectores.* These Himalayan crested irises are hardy but *I.tectorum* prefers a situation against a warm, sunny wall. Both are gross feeders and are best mulched with a rich compost in the spring.

I.milesii Foster (1893). Himalayas. The small, pink flowers, mottled-violet, are carried on well-branched stems, 100-125 cm (3 ft 3 ins-4 ft 1 in) tall. Individual flowers are short lived but a stem will flower for several weeks. The wide leaves form clumps from stout green rhizomes. A very worth-while general garden iris.

I.tectorum Maxim (1871). Central and S.W. China. Two deep lilac-blue flowers on a 40-cm (16 in) stem, occasionally branched. The leaves are a paler green. The albino form is specially beautiful. Tectorum has occasionally been hybridised with TBs.

2 (B) Lophiris. These dainty American irises are difficult to establish but once growing the short, green rhizomes spread rapidly. They do best in gritty soil in semi-shade. They can also be grown in a stone sink in a gritty compost should they fail in the open garden.

I.cristata Soland (1789). Georgia, Ohio, USA. Pale lavender flowers with a white patch and orange crest. 10 cm (4 ins) tall and almost stemless. There are many forms including an albino.

I.lacustris Nuttall (1818). Great Lakes, USA. Often classed as a very small form of *I.cristata*, this is one of the smallest of all irises, very dainty and charming.

I.tenuis Watson (1881). Oregon, USA. White flowers, veined blue, 30 cm (12 ins) tall. Transferred from the Californian series, this crested miniature is less hardy and more difficult to establish than the others in this series.

2 (C) Monospathae. The one eastern Asia species in this section grows in the same conditions as *I.cristata*.

I.gracilipes Gray (1858). Japan, China. This slender iris, with a much branched stem 15-20 cm (6-8 in) tall, has delightful, small, star-like lilac flowers. An albino form is not so robust. Both dislike being disturbed.

3. Sub-genus Limniris

The beardless rhizomatous irises. This sub-genus divides into five sections. The first, limniris, is the largest and is itself divided into four sub-sections. Of these, the apogon sub-section is split into twelve series or sub-series, the first seven being the smaller-leaved group, the next four the large-leaved, water-loving species while the last series has just one species.

3 (A) Limniris

Sub-section (I) *Apogon.*

(a) *Sibiricae.* These are plants from the well-watered meadows. They will grow well in most gardens although for full height and good stems they are best in a moist or bog garden. Unlike bearded irises they are best left to grow into large clumps. There are only two species.

I.sanguinea Donn (1811). Siberia, Korea, Manchuria, Japan. 100-cm (3 ft 3 in) stem, unbranched, with two terminal flowers. Blue-purple flowers and long, thin seed pods. The leaves are as tall but as they droop they appear shorter.

I.sibirica Linn (1753). West and south Europe, Russia, N.E. Turkey. 90-cm (3 ft) stem with one or two branches and up to five flowers, white to blue in colour, smaller than *I.sanguinea* and with short, stubby seed pods.

(b) *Chrysographes.* The eight species in this series were originally included in the sibiricae series but they do not hybridise with the sibiricae. They do, however, hybridise with the Californicae, forming the sterile Cal/Sib hybrids. They also like a damp, boggy position and do not like lime. They must not be allowed to dry out during growth or when being moved. They like a mulch around the plants but not over the shoots in spring and they are best left undisturbed.

I.bulleyana Dykes (1910). Could be a hybrid of *I.crysographes*. Blue-purple flowers with white/yellow markings on the falls, usually two to a stem. 45 cm (18 ins).

I.chrysographes Dykes (1911). Szechuan, Yunnan, upper Burma. Two deep red or even purple-black flowers on a 35-cm (14 in) stem, flowering above the thin leaves. The form with gold writing on its falls is a valuable bog plant.

I.clarkei Baker (1892). Nepal, Sikkim, Bhutan, Tibet, N.E. India, upper Burma. Flowers vary from blue to red-purple with a white patch on the haft of the falls. It has several flowers on a branched, solid stem 60 cm (2 ft) tall. The flowers appear above the 50-cm (20 in) broad leaves and distinguish this species from others in the series.

I.delavayi Micheli (1895). S.W. Szechuan, N. Yunnan. The last of this series to flower it is also the tallest with a 90-150-cm (3 ft-4 ft 11 in) stem with branching, each branch terminating with two deep-purple flowers with a white blaze on the falls. There is also a blue form.

I.dykesii Stapf (1932). This species was found in Dykes's garden after his tragic death and was named for him by Dr Stapf of Kew. It has been described as a 'super chrysographes' with violet-blue flowers with yellow signals. 80 cm (2 ft 8 ins).

I.forrestii Dykes (1910). N.W. Yunnan. One or two yellow flowers with black lines on the falls. Erect standards making the flowers taller than wide. 20-45-cm (8-18 in) stems with thin leaves shorter than the stems.

I.phragmitetorum Handel-Mazzetti (1925). N.W. Yunnan. A real bog lover. Dark-blue flowers with white patches on falls on stems 30-45 cm (12-18 ins) and with narrow leaves.

I.wilsonii Wright (1907). China, Hupei, Shan-si, Szechuan, Yunnan. Two yellow flowers with brown-black markings on falls. Standards at 45° so the flowers appear wider than tall. Stems 60 cm (2 ft) with leaves of the same length, but as they droop the flowers appear above them.

(c) *Prismaticae*. There is only one species in this series, the nearest American equivalent to *sibirica*. It does best in a damp or bog garden although it will grow in any rich loam which does not dry out. Rarely seen in cultivation, it is less temperamental than chrysographes.

I.prismatica Pursh (1814). Atlantic coast USA from N. Carolina to Maine. Very slender rhizomes, like 'couch grass' with two or three flowers, white veined blue and appearing as blue. 45-60-cm (18-24 in) stems. Very dainty as a flower arranger's flower.

(d) *Californicae*. The eleven species in this group require a lime-free soil and, with the exception of *I.innominata*, a semi-shaded, well-drained position. The bases of the leaves are usually coloured and turn red in the autumn.

I.bracteata Watson (1885). Siskiyou Mts, Oregon. Two pale yellow flowers on a 15-20-cm (6-8 in) stem.

I.chrysophylla Howell (1902). S. and Mid-west Oregon. Two flowers cream veined gold and violet. 20 cm tall.

I.douglasiana Herbert (1841). Coastal areas of S. Oregon and California. 20-30-cm (12-24 in) stems with up to nine flowers (2 or 3 from each spathe). Very variable in colour, purple, red, violet or white. Evergreen leaves 75 cm (2 ft 6 ins) tall. The best of the more robust species.

I.fernaldii Foster (1938). Sonoma Co. California. Two pale cream flowers on a 20-30-cm stem. Evergreen leaves.

I.hartwegii Baker (1876). Sierra Nevada Mts, California. Two creamy, yellow or lavender flowers on a 20-cm (8 in) stem. Pale green leaves.

> Sub-species *australis*. Leng (1958). San Gabriel Mts. California. Two violet-blue flowers.
> Sub-species *columbiana*. Leng (1957). Confined to a small area of Tuolumne Co. California. Three creamy yellow flowers veined gold on 30-40-cm (12-16 in) stem. A much more attractive plant than the species.
> Sub-species *pinetorum*. Leng (1958). Two creamy-yellow flowers veined gold both usually open together. 20 cm (8 ins). Could be a hybrid with *I.tenuissima*.

I.innominata Henderson (1930). S.W. Oregon, N.W. California. One, sometimes two flowers on a 10-20-cm (4-8 in) stem. They vary in colour from orange-buff to deep chrome yellow; from orchid-lavender to deep blue-purple, sometimes veined brown, red or purple. An ideal garden plant as it can be grown in more sun than the others in this group. Hybridises in the wild with *I.douglasiana* and is used in many hybridising programmes because of its narrow leaves.

I.macrosiphon Torrey (1857). Widespread in California. Two flowers, blue, lavender, purple, cream, yellow or white on a 25-cm (10 in) stem. Leaves evergreen without colour at the base.

I.munzii Foster (1938). Tulare Co. California. Two to four pale blue to purple flowers on a 50-60-cm (20-24 in) stem. Broad leaves up to 50 cm long. This species has the bluest form in the series but it tends to be tender and requires winter protection. Ideal for the bulb frame or alpine house.

I.purdyi Eastwood (1897). N. California. Two cream flowers, veined purple or rose on a 18-20-cm (7-8 in) stem. Evergreen.

I.tenax Douglas (1829). S.W. Washington. W. Oregon. One or occasionally two flowers deep purple shading through blue to white/yellow on a 25-30-cm (10-12 in) stem.

> Sub-species *klariathensis*. Leng (1958). One or two apricot to buff flowers veined red-brown on a 15-30-cm (6-12 in) stem. Evergreen.

I.tenuissima Dykes (1912). N. California. Two cream flowers veined purple or brown. 25-cm (10 in) stem. Evergreen.

> Sub-species *purdyiformis*. Leng (1958). N. Sierra Nevada. Two creamy-yellow flowers sometimes veined purple on a 25-cm stem.

The species in this series have given rise, in recent years, to many very colourful hybrids. As these hybrids are more widely grown so the true species from garden collected seed become more rare. Most hybrids are robust and well worth growing, the seed being sown where the plants are required to grow. They can be moved about four weeks after flowering. Wet sphagnum moss should be wrapped around the roots which must not be allowed to dry out and planting should be done with the moss still around the roots.

(e) *Tripetalae*. This series comprises three water-loving species from the old and the new world. Although water-loving they will grow in any good conditions and make ideal border or rock garden plants. They are best in lime-free conditions. They are used occasionally in hybrising with *I.sibirica* hybrids and the Californian series. It is also thought that they hybridise with *I.laevigata* in the wild. They are different from other irises in that the true petals (standards) have been reduced to thin ribs.

I.hookeri Penny (1829). Maritime eastern Canada. Often classed as a sub-species of *I.setosa*, this very delightful small iris has one or two flowers on a graceful 15-cm (6 in) stem.

135

I.setosa Pallas (1820). N.E. USSR, Manchuria, Korea, Japan, Alaska, N. Canada, Aleutian Islands. With so great a distribution there are many forms and a wide range of height. Up to 15 flowers are common on well branched stems (2-3) up to 30 cm (12 ins) tall. Flowers vary from pale blue-purple to purple. The leaves are not as tall as the flower stems.

I.tridentata Pursh (1814). Florida, Tennessee, N. and S. Carolina. One or two flowers on a 30-cm stem occasionally with one branch and one or two more flowers. Not always hardy in the UK but said to be so in the USA. Late flowering.

(f) *Longipetalae*. There is only one species in this series and, unlike those before, it is a lime lover. Its early flowering habit makes it an ideal garden plant.

I.missouriensis Nutt (1834). Wide range in western N. America. Up to five white or lavender-tinted flowers veined lilac-purple up to 75 cm (2 ft 6 ins) tall. Slender leaves shorter in most forms than the stems.

(g) *Chinensis*. Although six species are listed in this series only two are in cultivation. Others are said to exist in China and may be forms or new species. They resemble small sibiricas but are not hardy so would do best in a corner of the bulb frame where they could be watered during growth.

I.grijsii Maxim (1880). China. Two or three white flowers veined red purple. 5-20 cm (2-8 ins).

I.henryi Baker (1892). Szechuan. One yellow or lilac flower on a 5-20-cm stem.

I.koreana Nakai (1914). A yellow flower.

I.minutoaurea Makino (1928). Named from a species cultivated in Japan. One of the two species in cultivation although it does not often flower. One tiny yellow flower. 10 cm (4 ins).

I.polysticta Diels (1924). Szechuan. A pale lilac flower heavily spotted purple. 15-50 cm (6-20 ins).

I.rossii Baker (1877). Manchuria, Korea, Japan. The other species sometimes found in cultivation. A purplish-lilac flower on a 4-10-cm (1-4 in) stem.

(h) *Laevigatae*. The two species in this series are the true pond lovers. They have vigorous growing rhizomes and leaves and will stand a little lime. They are very good garden flowers.

I.laevigata Fischer (1837). Eastern Asia, China, Korea, Japan. Three or four pure blue flowers on a 35-40-cm (14-16 in) stem and in well-grown specimens a branch with two more flowers. The leaves have black 'watermarks' in the veins which is the way to tell the water-lovers from the bog plants.

I.pseudacorus Linn. (1753). Europe, Asia Minor, N. Africa. The 'yellow flag'. Well-branched stems up to 200 cm (6 ft 6 ins) tall with many yellow flowers. Cream and white flowers are sometimes found often with black-brown markings on falls. Leaves also have black 'watermarks'.

(i) *Kaempferi*. The one species in this series is usually classed in the laevigatae series but is distinct in that the seeds are a different shape, the leaves are heavily ribbed and without the watermark, it will not grow in water and does not like lime.

I.ensata Thumb (1794). Japan. Formerly known as *I.kaempferi*. Two or three deep purple flowers with a gold blaze on the falls. 60-cm (20 in) stems sometimes with one or two branches each with 2-3 flowers. The forerunner of the 'Japanese irises' now in many forms and colours. Extends the iris season to mid-summer.

(j) *Virginicae*. Also classed with the lacvigatae series, these two species are the American equivalent of our yellow flag. They are at home in the water or in the border and they do not mind a little lime. They are more vigorous in a wet than a dry garden border. The leaves have watermarks in them.

I.versicolor Linn. (1753). Eastern N. America from Hudson Bay to Texas. Up to nine flowers on a two or three-branched stem 60 cm (2 ft) tall. The blue or red-purple flowers have standards shorter than the falls and small, shiny seeds.

I.virginica Linn. (1753). Up to nine flowers on a two or three-branched stem 50-75 cm (20 ins-2 ft 6 ins) tall. The colour varies from blue to wine-red with standards as long as the falls and dull, cork-covered seeds. Not always as hardy as *I.versicolor*.

(k) *Hexagonae*. These are the Louisiana irises of the Mississippi swamps which are very showy, late flowering, waterside-garden irises. They require very heavy feeding and watering in spring, do best in swampy conditions and require a good winter mulch to protect them from the frost. All five species will grow in water but will not always take if planted in water. They have long, spreading, green rhizomes and require thinning to make them flower. They have zigzag stems with flowers at each bend which makes them very good flowers for floral art.

I.brevicaulis Rafinesque (1817). Mississippi basin. Three to six flowers usually violet-blue but variable on a zigzag stem 25-30 cm (10-12 ins) long. The leaves are 30-40 cm (12-20 ins) tall but the size and colour of the flowers make them clearly visible.

I.fulva Ker-Gawl (1812). Mississippi valley. Louisiana. Two copper-red flowers at the top of a 70-80-cm (2 ft 4 in-2 ft 8 in) stem with two more at joints, but stem does not zigzag as much as the others. Leaves 60-100 cm (2 ft-3 ft 3 ins) long.

I.giganticaerulea Small (1929). Gulf coast of Louisiana. Up to twelve blue to lavender flowers on a stem 70-100 cms (2 ft 4 ins-3 ft 3 ins) tall. Leaves about 60 cm (2 ft) long. Not so hardy as the others.

I.hexagona Walter (1788). E. states USA coastal regions. Up to twelve deep blue-purple flowers with a yellow mid rib on a 30-90-cm (1-3 ft) stem with leaves 60-90 cm. Not always hardy.

I.nelsonii Randolph (1966). Abbeville swamp, Louisiana. Up to ten red-purple, sometimes yellow flowers on an erect 70-100-cm stem with often 2-4 branches. Leaves not as tall — 80-90 cm (2 ft 8 ins-3 ft).

(l) *Vernae*. The beardless iris closest to the bearded. Has been hybridised with *I.pallida*. When established (which is not easy) and grown in a semi-shady, rich soil is very floriferous.

I.verna Linn. (1753). Pinewoods of Eastern USA. A lilac flower on a 5-cm (2 in) stem. Leaves about 10 cm (4 ins) at flowering time but grow taller after flowering time.

Sub-section (II) *Erimiris*

The single series in this sub-section, ensata, has a very confused taxonomy. The one species was originally named *I.ensata lactea* but *I.ensata* has now been transferred to *I.kaempferi*, which has ceased to exist. Many new names have been considered but it has not been established which was the earliest and should have precedence. We have, therefore, selected *I.lactea* as being most suitable for what we consider one of the best garden irises in cultivation.

I.lactea Pallas (1786). Central Asia, Kashmir, China, Korea.

A solitary, beautiful flower on a 10-30-cm (4-12 in) stem, dark standards and thin, delicate white falls heavily striated blue or red-purple. Requires a well-drained, rich loam.

Sub-section (III) *Tenuifoliae.*

Irises from this sub-section are not very common in cultivation. Possibly with the use of a bulb frame clones could be established. They need to be kept dry in winter and watered during the growing season. They have very fine rhizomes and do not like being disturbed.

(a) *Tenuifoliae.* Two species are known at present but more may be found to exist with study as they are not known in cultivation.

I.loczyi Kanitz (1891). China. Often classed as a form of *I.tenuifolia*. Two blue-purple flowers on a 15-cm (6 in) stem. Thin leaves 25 cm (10 ins) long.

I.tenuifolia Pallas (1773). Central China. Two blue-purple flowers on a 15-cm stem. Leaves 25 cm long.

(b) *Ventricosae.* Although placed in a different series, these two species have often been included as *I.tenuifolia*.

I.bungei Maximowicz (1880). Mongolia. Two pale-blue flowers with veined falls on an 8-16-cm (3-6 in) stem.

I.ventricosa Pallas (1773). River Argun between Siberia and Manchuria. A very rare and limited species, resembling *I.bungei* but with a few botanical differences.

Sub-section (IV) *Syriacae*

This division has only one species which comes from wet vernal spots in Asia Minor. The plant must have at least four months dry baking in the summer. If this condition could be provided it would do well in a small bulb frame which was watered in the autumn and winter when not too cold. It should be dried off in a bowl in summer.

I.grant-duffii Baker (1892). Asia Minor. A yellow flower, usually veined and spotted purple, on a 15-25-cm (6-10 in) stem. There are lilac and purple forms. The old leaves form bristles to protect the plants from grazing by animals.

3 (B) Unguiculares. The solitary species in this section is the winter-flowering iris from the Mediterranean area. It grows well in soil which is not too rich, in a sunny position against a south wall or in semi-shade. It does not like being moved and takes time to settle down. The flowers are best cut in the bud and brought into the house to open, when they will remain fresh and delightful for several days.

> *I.unguicularis* Poiret (1789). Algeria, Tunisia, N.E. Mediterranean. Two, often more, lilac flowers on a very short, almost undeveloped, stem. The flowers have a very long perianth tube, 5-20 cm (2-8 ins). The leaves are much longer than the flowers and many growers cut them back during the summer to allow the rhizomes to ripen. There are many varieties, few of which are named and the best are scented. Some start flowering in the late autumn, some in mid-winter and some in early spring. The form with small flowers and very thin leaves is often called *I.cretensis* and that with broad, drab-green leaves and dark-blue flowers which appear late is known as *I.lazica*. These are both collected clones.

3 (C) Ioniris.

Sub-section (I) *Ruthenicae*.

The single species can be associated with *I.verna* with regard to its habit but differs in many respects. It is distinguished by its pear-shaped seed which has a curious white appendage.

> *I.ruthenica* Ker-Gawl (1808). E. Europe, Russia, Mongolia, China. Usually two violet flowers marked white on the falls. Up to 10-cm (4 in) stems set in thin, grass-like foliage. An ideal species for the rock garden, in the sun or semi-shade and in moist or dry, rich loam.

3 (D) Xyridion.

Sub-section (I) *Xyridion*.

This section is sometimes classed with the apogon series and has also been put in a sub-genus of its own with the following section. We have left it in the sub-genus *Limniris* since all the species are beardless irises growing from rhizomes.

(a) *Spuriae*. The more robust species of this series are ideal for the wild garden. They will grow in any soil with plenty of humus, in the sun or semi-shade, in wet or dry conditions, lime or lime-free. The flowers resemble those of the Spanish and Dutch irises and are excellent for cutting.

> *I.brandzae* Prodan (1936). Romania, Bessarabia. Two blue-purple flowers on a 20-25-cm (8-10 in) stem. Thin leaves,

30-35 cm (12-14 ins) long.

I.carthaliniae Forin (1909). Caucasus, Transcaucasia, Georgia. Four or five sky-blue flowers, falls veined deeper blue usually with a yellow blaze. Flowers grouped at the end of a 95-cm (3 ft 2 in) stem. Leaves slightly longer.

I.crocea Jacquemont (1877). Kashmir. Up to six large golden yellow, wavy edged flowers on a 95-105-cm (3 ft 2 in-3 ft 5 in) stem. Leaves about 80 cm (2 ft 7 ins) only. A very handsome plant.

I.demetrii Arkv & Merz (1950). Transcaucasia, Armenia. Two to five dark violet-blue flowers on a 70-90-cm (2 ft 4in-3 ft) stem. Leaves 60-90 cm (2-3 ft).

I.halophila Pallas (1773). USSR. Four to eight flowers ranging in colour from white, yellowish to grey purple. Usually the white forms are the best. Stems 40-85 cm (16 ins-2 ft 9 ins) and leaves 30-60 cm (1-2 ft).

I.kerneriana Asch & Sint (1884). Asiatic Turkey, Armenia. Two deep-yellow flowers on a 25-cm (10 in) stem. Although the leaves are 30 cm long this is still a very desirable garden iris, better in the sun and when left undisturbed.

I.klattii Kemularia-Natadze (1949). N. Caucasus, Transcaucasia, USSR, Persia. Three to five violet-blue through grey-blue flowers with yellow blade on falls up to 50 cm (20 ins) tall. Similar to *I.notha* but coarser.

I.longipedicellata Czeczot (1932). Turkey, Galatea. Two pale-yellow flowers on a 30-40-cm (12-16 in) stem with leaves of the same length. Occasionally a side branch.

I.maritima Lamarck (1795). France, Corsica. Up to four deep-violet flowers on a 30-cm stem. Leaves as tall as the stem at flowering time but they grow taller after the flowers are over.

I.monnieri De Candolle (1808). Crete, Rhodes, Cilicia. Six or more pale-yellow flowers on a 75-100 cm (2 ft 6 in-3 ft 3 in) stem with leaves as tall as the stem. A very good garden flower.

I.notha M. Bieberstein (1843). Caucasus. Three to five violet-blue flowers with a yellow blaze on the falls. Up to 50-cm (20 in) stem.

I.orientalis Miller (1768). Asiatic Turkey. syn. *I.ochroleuca* Linn (1771). Four to nine large white flowers with yellow on the falls, 90-125 cm (3 ft-4 ft 1 in) tall. Leaves usually not quite as long. An ideal garden plant.

141

I.sintenisii Janka (1876). S. Italy, Balkans, Turkey, Asia Minor. One or two flowers on a 15-35-cm (6-14 in) stem. The falls are white, veined purple and the standards purple-blue. Leaves slightly longer.

I.sogdiana Bunge (1847). Central Asia. Not a very showy species. Small grey-lilac flowers on a 60-cm (2 ft) stem.

I.spuria Linn. (1753). Europe, Middle East, Central Asia. Up to ten flowers on a 50-cm (20 in) stem, the colour varying from violet to blue, yellow or white. Leaves as long as the stem. A very good garden plant.

I.uromovii Velonovsky (1902). Bulgaria. Two flowers, falls white veined and spotted deep blue and standards reddish on a 15-25-cm (6-10 in) stem. Thin leaves up to 30 cm (12 ins).

(b) *Gramineae*. Not so showy as the spuria series but they have good, plum-scented flowers which are usually hidden in the leaves.

I.graminea Linn. (1753). Central and Southern Europe, Turkey, Caucasus, Far East. One or two flowers with falls veined violet-blue on a pale ground and standards wine purple. Very sweetly scented. 10 to 60 cm (4-24 ins) tall according to form with leaves taller than the flowers.

I.ludwigii Maximowicz (1880). Altai Mts. One or two violet-blue flowers on a 10-20-cm (4-8 in) stem. Distinguished from all other Limniris by having a hairy beard on the falls. Leaves 40 cm (16 ins) tall.

I.pontica Zapalowicz (1906). USSR, Caucasia. One or two large, scented flowers 10-20-cm stem. Falls white or cream, veined purple, standards pale blue.

3 (E) Spathula. This is a name often used for most of the *Limniris* but as *I.foetidissima* is on its own it fits best in this section.

Sub-section (I) *Foetidissima*.

I.foetidissima Linn. (1753). Western Europe, N.W. Africa. This is one of our native irises and is a very useful plant for almost all growing conditions. It has very dark, glossy leaves with up to three inconspicuous flowers which can be mauvish, creamy-white or yellow on stems 35-45 cm (14-18 ins) tall. The plant is most useful for floral art as in the winter the seed capsules split open and curl down to reveal brilliant red or red-orange berries.

4. Sub-genus Nepalensis

The species in this sub-genus come from the Himalayas and Yunnan and are distinct in having roots like those of Hemerocallis (Day Lily). Coming from a near-monsoon climate they require six months drying out and plenty of water during growth. They do best in a semi-shady spot in a bulb frame, being given a rich mulch and plenty of water in the spring. They can be grown in the bog garden and they dislike being moved.

> *I.collettii* Hooker (1909). N. Burma, Thailand, Yunnan. Three to seven lilac-blue flowers on a 5-15-cm (2-6 in) stem. Leaves coarser than those of *I.decora*.

> *I.decora* Wallick (1832). Western Central Himalayas into Yunnan. Three to seven lilac-blue flowers on a 15-37-cm (6-15 in) stem. Leaves about 30 cm (12 ins) at flowering time increasing to 45-60 cm (18-24 ins) after flowering.

5. Sub-genus Pardanthopsis

The single species is known as the 'Vesper Iris' and bears many delightful small flowers which last only a few hours, but the flowering period extends from late summer to autumn. Masses of seeds are then produced and the exhausted plant then usually dies. Raising from seed is easy and the plant will do well in a well-drained soil in full sun or in a bulb frame.

> *I.dichotoma* Pallas (1773). Siberia, China, Manchuria, Japan. Many butterfly-like flowers, lilac or pinkish, on a 60-80-cm (2 ft-2 ft 8 in) stem.

6. Sub-genus Xiphium

This first group of bulbous irises mostly require a sunny, well-drained position. They make good cut flowers. They have been selected and hybridised to produce the Spanish and Dutch irises which are grown commercially for sale as cut flowers.

> *I.boissieri* Henriques (1885). N. Portugal, N.W. Spain. Usually a single violet-purple flower 30 cm (12 ins) tall. Unique in that it has a yellow beard on the falls. The leaves appear in spring. Best grown in a large bulb frame.

> *I.filifolia* Boissier (1842). S.W. Spain, Gibraltar, Morocco, Tangier. One, but more often, two reddish-violet flowers with a yellow patch on the falls. 25-45 cm (10-18 ins) tall. Leaves appear in autumn. Best in a cold house or bulb frame.

> *I.juncea* Poiret (1789). S. Spain, Sicily, N. Africa. Two fragrant, yellow flowers on a 30-cm stem. Leaves appear in autumn. Best in a bulb frame.

I.latifolia Miller (1768). (*I.xiphioides*) N.W. Spain, Pyrenees. Two or three purple, blue or white flowers on a 45-cm (18 in) stem. Leaves appear in the spring. This species is known as the 'English iris', is hardy and is the only one in this section which will grow in shade or semi-shade. It requires more water than most.

I.serotina Willk (1861). S.E. Spain. One or two violet-blue flowers with a yellow blaze on the falls and reddish standards on a 40-60-cm (16-24 in) stem. Leaves appear in autumn and die off before flowering. Best in a bulb frame or a sheltered, sunny, dry border.

I.tingitana Boiss & Reut (1853). Morocco, Algeria. One to three blue flowers on a 40-60-cm stem. Leaves appear in the autumn.

I.xiphium Linn. (1753). Spain, Portugal, Morocco, Corsica, S. Italy. One or two flowers on a 40-60-cm stem. Colours vary according to variety: *xiphium* — blue, mauve or violet; *battandieri* — white; *praecox* — early and extra large; *taitii* — pale blue. All with a yellow or orange blaze. Hardy in well-drained, sunny positions. These gave rise to the Spanish and Dutch irises. Leaves appear in autumn.

7. Sub-genus Iridodictyum

Sub-section (I) *Reticulatae.*

These net-covered bulbous irises enjoy water during growth but not while dormant. They need a dry, sunny spot or a bulb frame.

(a) *Reticulatae.*

I.bakerana Foster (1889). Turkey, W. Iran, E. Iraq. A single, scented, blue-violet flower with white markings on the falls, about 5 cm (2 ins) tall. Round leaves with eight veins appear with the flowers but grow much taller after flowering. After flowering the bulbs tend to split into two or three fairly large flowering bulbs.

I.danfordiae Baker (1876). S. Central Turkey. A deep-yellow, funnel-shaped flower with reduced standards and spotted in brown on the blade of the falls. 2-5 cm (1-2 ins). The four-sided leaves are not as tall as the flowers at flowering time but increase in height afterwards. The bulbs break down to 'rice' size after flowering and these require plenty of feeding to grow to flowering size. Often referred to as an annual.

I.histrio Reichenbach (1872). S. Turkey, Syria, Lebanon, Israel. Pale-blue flowers with falls dotted in grey-purple.

3-5 cm (1¼-2 ins). Leaves four-sided and square 15-20 cm (5-8 ins) tall at flowering time and increasing later. Bulbs increase by 'rice' bulblets at the base.

I.histrioides Foster (1893). N. Central Turkey. Large, blue flowers blotched deeper blue. 3-5 cm. Flowers appear before the square-section leaves which grow later. The bulbs produce 'rice' grains at base.

I.hyrcana Woronow (1928). Caucasus. Clear blue flowers on 2-cm (1 in) stems. Four-sided leaves about 2 cm taller than flowers but increasing later. Spherical bulbs with many bulblets.

I.pamphylica Hedge (1961). Taurus Mts. S. Turkey. Slender flowers on a 10-cm (4 in) stem. Falls olive or brown and standards pale blue dappled brown-grey. Slender leaves 30 cm (12 ins) at flowering time.

I.reticulata M.Bieberstein (1808). E. Turkey, S. Caucasus, Iran. Scented, blue or violet flowers on 3-cm (1¼ in) stems. Four-sided leaves 30 cm tall at flowering time which can grow to 75 cm (2 ft 6 ins) later. Bulbs produce large bulblets after flowering. Many named forms and hybrids.

I.vartanii Foster (1885). Israel, S. Syria. Scented slaty-blue or white flowers on tiny stems, 3 cm. Four unequal-sided leaves 20 cm (8 ins) tall at flowering time but growing to double the height later. Bulbs increase by growing 'rice' grain bulblets.

I.winogradowii Fomin (1914). Transcaucasia. Yellow flowers on a 5-cm (2 in) stem. Like *I.histrioides* the flowers appear before the four-sided leaves which grow to 45 cm (18 ins) later. Slow to increase.

(b) *Monlepsis*. The plants in this series differ from the reticulatas in having somewhat flattened, crocus-like leaves.

I.kolpakowskiana Regel (1877). USSR. Blue-purple or white flowers on 5-cm stems. Few leaves, 5 cm at flowering time but increasing to 30 cm (12 ins) later.

I.winkleri Regel (1884). S. Russia. Similar to *I.kolpakowskiana* but the bulb has a membranous, not netted, covering.

8. Sub-genus Scorpiris

The plants in this group have fleshy roots which should not be broken off. They have leaves like miniature sweetcorn. The flowers have reduced standards, often reflex, and many are also scented. Few are hardy and will do best if grown in a bulb frame or in deep bowls in an alpine house. The bulbs should be planted 10 cm (4 ins) deep and a rich mulch is needed each year. The group is divided into three sections and two series.

8 (A) **Juno.** Plants with stems with the flowers appearing in the leaf axils.

I.aitchisonii Bois (1884). W. Pakistan, E. Afghanistan. One to three lilac-purple flowers with winged falls, 30-60 cm (1-2 ft). A yellow-bronze form has been reported.

I.albomarginata Foster (1936). USSR, Central Asia. Two to five bluish-mauve or blue flowers on a short stem. 37 cm (15 ins) tall.

I.almaatensis Pavlov (1950). USSR, Central Asia.

I.atropatana Grossch (1936). USSR, Central Asia. Two or three yellow flowers. 10-15 cm (4-6 ins).

I.aucheri Baker (1877). W. Iran. N. Iraq, N. Syria. Up to six smoky grey-blue flowers. 15-23 cm (6-9 ins).

I.bucharica Foster (1902). N. Afghanistan, USSR, C. Asia. Up to seven creamy-yellow flowers. 30-45 cm (12-18 ins). One of the few hardy species for a sheltered spot.

I.caucasica Hoffman (1808). USSR, Transcaucasia, N. Iraq, N.W. Iran, S. Turkey. One to four pale yellow flowers with winged falls. 5-15 cm (2-6 ins). Leaves developed at flowering time. The variety Kharput does not have winged falls.

I.cycloglossa Wendelbo (1958). W. Afghanistan. One to three pale, lilac-blue flowers on a branched stem up to 60 cm (2 ft) tall. Unique among Junos in having larger upright standards and broad, winged falls. Comes from wet grassland and so could need more water than other Junos.

I.edomensis Sealy (1950). Transjordan. One or two whitish flowers spotted purple. Up to 12 cm (5 ins). In affinity with *I.albomarginata*.

I.eleonorae Holmboe (1907). C. Turkey. One or two purple flowers up to 5 cm (2 ins). Close to *I.persica*.

I.fosterana Aitch & Baker (1888). USSR, N.E. Iran, N.W. Afghanistan, Turkey. One or two creamy-yellow flowers, not winged. 30-cm (12 in) stem. Thin leaves and small, fleshy roots. Cubical seeds being similar to *xiphium*.

I.graeberana Sealy (1950). USSR, C. Asia. Four to six pale, silvery-mauve flowers, up to 45 cm (18 ins). One of the more vigorous, hardy species.

I.hymenospatha Mathew & Wendelbo (1975). W. Iran, E. Iraq. A creamy-white winged flower on a short stem up to 5 cm (2 ins). Close to *I.persica*.

I.linifolia Fedtsch (1905). USSR, C. Asia. One or two pale, greenish-yellow flowers up to 15 cm (6 ins) tall. Seed with white aril.

I.magnifica Vvedensky (1935). C. Asia. Up to seven pale-violet flowers on a 60-cm (2 ft) stem. Robust and hardy in a warm, sheltered spot.

I.maracandica Wendelbo (1935). C. Asia. One to four pale-yellow flowers up to 18 cm (7 ins).

I.microglossa Wendelbo (1958). N. Central Afghanistan. Two pale white-mauve flowers with wings. 5-6 cm (2-2½ ins).

I.narbuti O. Fedtschenko (1950). USSR, C. Asia. One or two greenish-yellow flowers with pale violet falls. Up to 5-10 cm (2-4 ins).

I.narynensis O.Fedtschenko (1905). USSR, C. Asia. One or two dark-violet flowers up to 7 cm (3 ins).

I.odontostyla Mathew & Wendelbo (1975). N.W. Afghanistan. One greyish-violet winged flower with an orange-yellow crest. 13 cm (5 ins).

I.orchioides Carr (1880). USSR, C. Asia. Three to six pale and deep-yellow flowers. 30 cm (12 ins). Differs from *I.bucharica* in having winged falls.

I.parvula Vvedensky (1935). USSR, C. Asia. Greenish-yellow flowers with green veining. Up to 10 cm (4 ins).

I.persica Linn. (1753). Iran, Iraq, Turkey. One or two flowers with winged falls up to 5 cm (2 ins). The colour varies from greenish-blue, pale yellow, creamy-white, purple, grey-blue. Often with a deeper blotch on the falls.

I.pseudocaucasica Grossheim (1916). N.W. Iran, USSR, Transcaucasia. Up to four pale-blue flowers with winged falls. Up to 13 cm (5 ins).

I.stocksii Baker (1884). Afghanistan. One to four pale violet-blue flowers with winged falls. 25-30 cm (10-12 ins).

I.subdecolorata Vvedensky (1923). USSR, C. Asia. One to three greenish-lilac flowers on very short stems, only up to 3 cm (1¼ ins) tall.

I.tadshikorum Vvedensky (1935). USSR, C. Asia. Two to four pale-violet flowers on a 10-cm (4 in) stem.

I.tauri Siehe (1901). Turkey. One or two dark-violet, purple-winged flowers up to 5 cm (2 ins). Very close to *I.persica*.

I.tubergeniana Foster (1899). USSR, C. Asia. One to three deep-yellow, winged flowers on a short stem, usually underground.

I.vicaria Vvedensky (1935). C. Asia. One to four violet flowers with stems up to 30-37 cm (12-15 ins) tall.

I.vvedenskyi Nevski (1932). C. Asia. One or two light-yellow flowers 5 cm (2 ins) tall.

I.warleyensis Foster (1902). USSR, C. Asia. Three to five pale, violet-mauve flowers without wings and with strap-like falls. 45 cm (18 ins). Seed cubical. Hardy in a warm spot.

I.willmottiana Foster (1901). C. Asia, E. Turkestan. Four to six flowers with winged falls, usually blue to blue-purple. Up to 15 cm (6 ins).

8 (B) Physolcaulon. The plants in this section have thickened stems at the base and usually flower before the stems are fully developed.

(a) *Drepanophylla.* This series has stems with the nodes developed, whereas in the series Rosenbachianae the internodes are very close together. They also have different types of pollen.

I.carterorum Mathew & Wendelbo (1975). C. Afghanistan. Two flowers with purple, black-spotted falls and greenish-yellow standards. 7 cm (3 ins).

I.drepanophylla Aitch & Baker (1888). N.E. Iran, N.W. Afghanistan. Up to twelve yellow-green flowers without wings, up to 30 cm (12 ins) tall. Seed with white aril.

I.kopetdaghensis Vvedensky (1935). N.E. Iran, USSR, C. Afghanistan. Up to nine greenish-yellow flowers without wings on falls on stem 15-30 cm (6-12 ins). Seed with white aril.

I.porphyrochrysa Wendelbo (1969). N. Afghanistan. One to three brownish-purple flowers with a yellow crest, up to 10 cm (4 ins) tall.

I.xcanthochlora Wendelbo (1969). C. Afghanistan. One to three yellowish-green flowers with small wings, 15 cm tall. Leaves are complete at flowering time. Could be related to *I.linifolia*.

I.wendelboi Grey-Wilson & Mathew (1974). S.W. Afghanistan. One or two deep-violet blue, wingless flowers. 9-12 cm (4-5 ins).

(b) *Rosenbachianae.*

I.baldschuanica Fedtschenko (1909). China, Turkestan. One to three yellowish flowers veined purple. Maximum height 10 cm (4 ins), usually less. Differs from *I.rosenbachiana* in having leaves more developed at flowering time.

I.cabulica Gilli (1954). Kabul, Afghanistan. One to three pale-lilac-white flowers stem 3 cm (1¼ ins) at flowering time, increasing to 10 cm (4 ins). Leaves sickle-shaped. Seeds pear-shaped with aril.

I.doabensis Mathew (1972). Afghanistan. One to three yellow flowers on a 10-cm stem which grows longer after flowering.

I.nicolai Vvedensky (1935). USSR. One or two pale-rose flowers with purple blotch on a stem up to 10 cm. Close to *I.rosenbachiana* but early flowering. Seed with aril.

I.platyptera Mathew & Wendelbo (1975). W. Afghanistan, W. Pakistan. Two to three flowers, pale or dark purple-violet with a yellow crest. 8-14 cm (3-6 ins).

I.popovii Vvedensky (1935). C. Asia. Two to four violet-blue flowers up to 10 cm.

I.rosenbachiana Regel (1884). N. Afghanistan, USSR, C. Asia. One to three pale-mauve flowers with a purple blotch on a 10-cm (4 in) stem. Flowers later than *I.nicolai*. Seed with aril.

I.zaprjagajewii Abramov (1971). USSR, C. Asia. One or two pure-white flowers with a yellow crest. 0-5 cm (2 ins) tall. Seed with aril.

8 (C) Acanthospora. Like those in the Juno section, these plants have well-developed stems. They appear to differ only in their pollen.

I.palaestina Boiss (1884). Israel, Syria, Lebanon, Jordan. Up to three greenish, grey-white flowers, with winged falls up to 7 cm (3 ins) tall. Tender and a poor grower.

I.planifolia Ascherson (1864). S. Europe, Sicily, Sardinia, Spain, N. Africa. Up to three silvery-mauve flowers with winged falls, up to 7 cm tall. Tender and does not flower every year in cultivation.

I.postii Mouterde (1966). Iraq, E. Jordan, E. Syira. One to four blotched violet flowers on a 10-20-cm (4-10 in) stem.

Note. There are a number of other species in this sub-genus which have not been classified.

9. Sub-genus Gynandriris

Rootstock is a corm (swollen stem), instead of a bulb, which is netted like the reticulata section. One species from the Cape and the other from Europe and Asia. Needs full sun.

> *I.setifolia* Linn. (1753). Often classed as a Moraea because it comes from the Cape, S. Africa. Short-lived blue flowers. 15 cm (6 ins) tall.

> *I.sisyrinchium* Linn. (1753). France, Portugal, Morocco, eastwards to N.W. India. Up to twenty short-lived flowers giving a succession of blue flowers. 5-20 cm (2-8 ins). Produces lateral sheathes of flowers as well as terminal.

10. Sub-genus Hermodactylus

Rootstock is a tuber instead of a bulb or rhizome. Leaves quadrangular like the reticulata section. Hardy in a rich, sunny spot against a south wall or in a bulb frame.

> *I.tuberosa* Linn. (1753). S. France, Italy, N. Africa, Greece, Albania, Jugoslavia. The 'Widow Iris' with one flower with velvet-black falls and green standards. 15-30-cm (6-12 in) stem. Sweetly scented. Leaves grow very long after flowering.

Note. This is not intended as a truly botanical classification. It has been composed from different classifications and we hope that most names above species level have been incorporated as a guide to the different classifications. For example, to be strictly botanical, the first sub-genus would read *Iris*, section Iris, sub-section Iris and the intermediate bearded would also be called Iris. This is because *I.germanica* (no longer a valid species) was the type plant first described as an iris.

We have used as a guide *The Genus Iris*, W.R. Dykes; *The World of Irises*, AIS (with the Lawrence classification); the BIS *Year Books*; *The Genus Iris*, Dr Rodionenko for his classification and the *Catalogus Iridis* by P. Werckmeister. For species names we have relied on the BIS *Year Books*, *The World of Irises* and the *Notes* of the Species Group of the BIS. We acknowledge, also, the considerable help of Steven Jury of Reading University.

We have not dealt with synonyms as they would have needed more time and space than was available. The best published list will be found in the *Catalogus Iridis* by P. Werckmeister.

In recent times there has been a tendency to reduce the scope of the genus *Iris*. In some classifications, for example, the sub-genus *Gynandriris* has been put in a genus of its own, with some of the *Moraeas* included as they come from tropical Africa. The sub-genus *Hermodactylus* has also been taken out. Dr Rodionenko has promoted the sub-genera *Xiphium*, *Iridodictyum* and *Scorpiris* (Juno) to genus status. In America the sub-genus *Pardanthopsis* has also been up-graded.

As the world becomes more intensively cultivated, so the natural plant habitats tend to disappear. The conservation of flora is more and more in the hands of enthusiastic amateurs. We think it is better to increase rather than reduce the scope of the genus *Iris* in the hope that the many specialised iris societies around the world will be pleased to take the additional species into their care and especially protect those which are threatened. In time, perhaps, the genus may be further extended to include the *Moraea*, *Herbertia*, *Dietes*, *Trimezia* and other related genera, with more botanical sections to show their differences.

Bibliography

The American Iris Society. *Alphabetical Iris Check Lists*. 1939, 1949, 1959, 1969 and annually.

The American Iris Society. (ed. B. Warburton), *The World of Irises*, 1978.

Anley, G. *Irises, their Culture and Selection*, 1926.

Baker, J.G. *Handbook of the Irideae*, 1892.

Berrisford J. *Irises*, 1961.

The British Iris Society. *Year Book*, annually.

The British Iris Society. *An Alphabetical Table and Cultivation Guide to the Species of the Genus Iris*, 1974.

Cave, N.L. *The Iris*, 1959.

Dykes, W.R. *The Genus Iris*, 1913. (Facsimile edn, Dover Books, 1975).

Dykes, W.R. *Handbook of Garden Irises*, 1924.

Foster, Sir M. *Bulbous Irises*, 1892.

Lynch, R.I. *The Book of the Iris*, 1904.

Mathew, B. *The Iris*, 1981.

Mitchell, S.B. *Iris for Every Garden*, 1949.

Moore, N. *The Tall Bearded Iris*, 1956.

Price, M. *The Book of the Iris*, 1966.

Pesel, L.F. and Spender, R.H.S. *Iris Culture for Amateurs*, 1937.

Randall H. *Irises*, 1969.

Randolph, L.F. *Garden Irises*, 1959.

Rockwell, F.F. *Irises*, 1928.

Rodionenko, G.I. *The Genus Iris*, 1961 (in Russian).

Ross, W. *Iris, Goddess of the Garden*, 1966.

Shull, J.M. *Rainbow Fragments*, 1911.

Stevens, J. *The Iris and its Culture*, 1950.

Vallette W. *Iris Culture and Hybridizing for Everyone*, 1961.

Wister, J.C. *The Iris*, 1927.

Wendelbo, P. and Mathew, B. *Iridaceae in Flora Iranica*, 1975.

Werckmeister, P. *Catalogus Iridis*, 1967.

Glossary

Amoena	An iris with white, or nearly white, standards and coloured falls.
Anther	The pollen-bearing part of the stamen.
Apogon	Irises which have no beard or crest.
Aril	A small white or cream appendage or collar on some iris seeds.
Beard	The line of hairs growing from the haft of the falls of some irises.
Bicolour	An iris having standards and falls of different colours.
Blade	The wide part of the standard or fall of an iris flower.
Chromosome	The body in the cell nucleus bearing the genes.
Crest	(a) The two points at the outer end of the style arm.
	(b) In Evansia irises the raised, serrated ridge along the centre of the falls.
Cross	(a) Verb. To transfer pollen from one flower to the stigma of another.
	(b) Noun. Loose term for the seedling resulting from such cross pollination.
Cultivar	A cultivated variety.
Diploid	Having two sets of chromosomes.
Domed	Standards when rounded and closed.
Embryo	The tiny life-point within a seed which grows into a seedling on germination.
Eupogon	True bearded.
Falls	The three outer petals of an iris flower.
Flared	Term applied to falls which are held horizontally or near horizontally.
Gene	Unit of heredity.
Genus	Taxonomic group of species with common characteristics.
Haft	The lower, narrow part of the petals of an iris.
Hybrid	Seedling raised by crossing two or more species.
Neglecta	An iris with light-blue standards and dark-purple falls.
Ovary	The seed case below the perianth tube which bears the seed pod.
Perianth tube	The tube connecting the flower and the ovary.
Plicata	An iris having a light background with veining and dotting of a darker colour.
Pogoniris	A bearded iris.
Pollen	The fine grains carried on the anthers which bear the male germ cells.
Regeliocyclus	Hybrid irises obtained by crossing Regelia and Oncocyclus irises.
Rhizome	The thick, fleshy root or horizontal stem from which the leaves

grow upwards and the roots downwards.

Ruffled Term applied to petals which are waved at the edges.

Signal A distinctive coloured blotch on the haft of the falls.

Species A group of plants which are botanically distinct.

Stamen The male reproductive organ consisting of the anther and the filament.

Standards The three inner petals of an iris.

Stigma Small outgrowth on the style which becomes sticky and to which pollen grains adhere.

Style Part of the flower which extends from the ovary and bears the stigma.

Tetraploid Having four sets of chromosomes.

Triploid Having three sets of chromosomes.

Index

GENERAL

Index

SPECIES AND COLLECTED FORMS

Index

CULTIVARS

Index